Tenkin and Career Management in a Changing Japan

Tenkin and Career Management in a Changing Japan

Noriko Fujita

LEXINGTON BOOKS
Lanham • Boulder • New York • London

Published by Lexington Books
An imprint of The Rowman & Littlefield Publishing Group, Inc.
4501 Forbes Boulevard, Suite 200, Lanham, Maryland 20706
www.rowman.com

86-90 Paul Street, London EC2A 4NE

Copyright © 2024 by The Rowman & Littlefield Publishing Group, Inc.

All rights reserved. No part of this book may be reproduced in any form or by any electronic or mechanical means, including information storage and retrieval systems, without written permission from the publisher, except by a reviewer who may quote passages in a review.

British Library Cataloguing in Publication Information Available

Library of Congress Cataloging-in-Publication Data

Names: Fujita, Noriko, author.
Title: Tenkin and career management in a changing Japan / Noriko Fujita.
Description: Lanham : Lexington Books, [2024] | Includes bibliographical references and index. | Summary: "Drawing on the rich, qualitative-interview-based data from Japanese firms and dual-career workers, the author discusses Tenkin, cultural and gendered corporate transfers, workers' agency, and argues the need to incorporate the concept of care in career management" —Provided by publisher.
Identifiers: LCCN 2024028460 (print) | LCCN 2024028461 (ebook) | ISBN 9781793604378 (cloth) | ISBN 9781793604385 (epub)
Subjects: LCSH: Career development—Japan. | Personnel management—Japan.
Classification: LCC HF5382.5.J3 F85 2024 (print) | LCC HF5382.5.J3 (ebook) | DDC 331.7020952—dc23/eng/20240628
LC record available at https://lccn.loc.gov/2024028460
LC ebook record available at https://lccn.loc.gov/2024028461

Contents

Acknowledgments	vii
Introduction: *Tenkin* as the Subject	1
1 The Practice Taken for Granted	31
2 Development and Changes in the Practice?	57
3 Young Workers and *Salariiman*	65
4 Dual-Career Couples Living Apart	77
5 Dual-Career Couples Collaborating	101
Conclusion: Career Management in Contemporary Japan	135
Appendix A: The Firms Interviewed by the Author	143
Appendix B: The Individuals Interviewed by the Author	145
Bibliography	151
Index	159
About the Author	161

Acknowledgments

This book is, first and foremost, indebted to all the informants who generously participated in this research. I am truly thankful to all of them for sharing their experiences of *tenkin* as individual employees, spouses, and also, as HR managers of large companies. Even after our interviews, some of them stayed in touch with me over emails and allowed me to follow-up on their lives. Some introduced a number of interviewees to me using their personal networks. Without their cooperation and understanding in my research, I could never be able to reach this point of writing up this book. It is sincerely a pity that I cannot reveal their names here one by one, as that would violate research ethics, but again, I would like to thank them very much for everything they have given to this research.

Yet, among them, my special thanks go to some of my acquaintances and friends who listened to my ideas for this research and helped me obtain access to interviewees. They are Professor Ikegami, Ms. Kondo, Ms. Hosoi, Ms. Miwa, Mr. Yahiro, and Ms. Hiramatsu. Ms. Masako Hiramatsu, past president of a non-government organization, *National Federation of Business and Professional Women's Clubs of Japan* (BPW-Japan), was always supportive of me, understanding my passion for gender equality, since I had participated in an internship for the 48th Commission on the Status of Women in the United Nations in 2004. My friends from Sophia University and their husband and friends also helped me find individual interviewees. Besides, their real-life based critical and humorous insights have always pushed me to pursue my academic interests in Japanese society.

Almost all the expenses for conducting this research were funded by the Murata Foundation for 2015. Interview-based qualitative research generally requires a lot of time, as well as generous funding. In my case, transportation fees were considerably expensive, since my interviewees were situated in various cities in Japan. This fund also allowed me to provide a small gift for the interviewees, as is the custom in Japan, or as well to pay for their meals, if the interview was held over lunch. Without the grant by the Murata Foundation, I could not have held the interviews which form the backbone of narratives in this book.

The intellectual development of this thesis was guided by Professor Scott North at Osaka University. After I finished the doctoral program in Waseda University in March 2017, I joined North-sensei's graduate seminar and international labor theory class. There, I was trained to have a critical view on contemporary work, employment, labor, and family issues. North-sensei not only provided me with a number of thoughtful comments on the arguments in this book but also taught me how to write a thesis, or more precisely, how to tackle with writing it up. Thanks to his advice, I was able to stay writing my dissertation, which was the original draft of this book, without burning myself out.

In terms of English writing, I would like to give my sincere appreciation to my former teacher at Kariya High School, Ikuta Shōzō-sensei, for teaching me the basics of writing. His college-style lectures were always stimulating, and the three full years in his class was the base of my lifelong interests and efforts in improving my language skills.

I am grateful to sociologist, Professor Gracia Liu-Farrer. Her feedback on my project from critical views was always thoughtful and encouraging. I also learned how to perform interviews from Farrer-sensei at our joint fieldwork for the Deutscher Akademischer Austauschdienst project in February 2017. Her enthusiasm for pursuing academic research was an inspiration.

Finally, my deepest gratitude goes to my mentor, Professor Glenda S. Roberts at Waseda University. After acquiring a bachelor's degree in German Literature in Sophia, I was looking for a place to study more deeply about human beings. She taught me that I could find answers to my queries by studying anthropology and gender and led me to Japanese studies during the two years of the master's course. She welcomed me to the doctoral course after I took the exit option from my previous job. In the beginning of the course, I was devastated by the fact that I had lost almost all the knowledge I had accumulated during my MA. Glenda-sensei patiently and enthusiastically spent her time with me and intellectually supported and encouraged me in every part of my research. After I earned the Ph.D., we began co-research on labor migration issues in Japan's agricultural field. Over these three years, I broadened my perspectives, which led me to delving into another research subject. I sincerely appreciate her guidance.

Last but not least, I have been given full encouragement by my family. My mother Hiroko Kutsuna has always believed in me, encouraged me with her great sense of humor, and supported me. My husband Junya Fujita has been a strong supporter of me as well. I am fond and proud of the journey, full of challenges and adventures, we made as researchers as well as life partners.

Introduction

Tenkin *as the Subject*

WHY *TENKIN*?

Tenkin stands for corporate transfers. I use the Japanese word to illuminate its cultural meaning, which has been seldom discussed. *Tenkin* is different from *tenshoku*, the practice of changing companies or jobs. People, including my informants in this study, tend to find it difficult to explain the difference. This is fundamental because they were rarely able to explain what *tenkin* is. At least between 2014 and 2017 when I was carrying out the fieldwork, there was little shared sense of the meaning, function, and purpose of *tenkin* in Japanese society, despite the prevalence of the word and the challenges that people encounter in their work and family lives.

Japanese *tenkin* is distinctive by its compulsoriness and embeddedness in society. *Tenkin* is a mandate practice and workers have little discretion, as I myself went through it three times while I was working for a private company. In workplaces in Europe and the United States, for example, when some workers are requested to be transferred somewhere, they are given discretion and time to consider it. They may bring the offer to their home and discuss with family members whether or not they accept it. But *tenkin* is by and large mandatory. Japanese workers are supposed to respond to it only with a simple "yes" answer, and furthermore, if it is a domestic *tenkin*, they have to be ready for a move within a few days, and people take it for granted. Why is that so? If workers are dual-career couples with small children, how do they balance their work and family lives? I came to question that way and this motivated me to study the practice of *tenkin*. Through the lens of *tenkin* we can view how couples in dual-career families are experiencing and experimenting with their work and family lives in Japan's changing corporate environment and society.

In 2022, the Cabinet Office of Japan held a study group on "Women and Economy" (Nagase 2022). Professor Nobuko Nagase at Ochanomizu Women's University reported that the reform of the working styles and social security system is necessary to tackle the fertility and demographic decline. In particular, she emphasized the need to reform the nationwide *tenkin* system. She noted the reason that if workers have a job that necessitates them to be transferred even during their reproductive years, they have to have a full-time homemaker who can assume the responsibilities of the domestic sphere. In other words, *tenkin* is not compatible with the dual-career couples' model (Nagase 2022).

Before the Cabinet Office study group, only scant scholarly attention had been paid to the importance of *tenkin*. Sociologists Meguro and Shibata (1999) noted that *tenkin* is a corporate-centered practice, which stands on the premise of the male-breadwinner model and influences family lives negatively. Miyoshi (2009) focused on *tenkin* of dual-career couples and revealed that whichever member of the couple is transferred, it becomes a roadblock for the women's career development. Anthropologists Sawa Kurotani (2005) and Blaine Phillip Connor (2010) also argued through their ethnographic studies on the consciousness of people that *tenkin* forces a couple into a strictly gendered division of labor. Kurotani (2005) found that the wives of corporate husbands who were transferred to the United States due to their *tenkin* tended to follow their husbands to maintain their "home away from home." In the home, the wives willingly fulfilled the domestic roles, seeing it indispensable to enable the husbands to give full physical and psychological commitment to their work. Connor's (2010) study on public school teachers' *tenkin* in Nagasaki Prefecture found that married female teachers, who tried to achieve their career through periodic and mandatory *tenkin* between cities and islands within the prefecture, faced work/life conflicts as public servants, wives, and mothers, due to their primary responsibility as caregivers. To put it otherwise, *tenkin* has embodied the gender division of labor in both employment and family in Japan.

Meanwhile, the Japan Institute for Labour Policy and Training (JILPT 2017) conducted a comprehensive study on *tenkin*, paying attention to both corporate practices and workers' consciousness. To begin with, 78.2 percent of Japanese firms with 1,000 employees and more conducted *tenkin* in 2016 (JILPT 2017: 5). The major purpose for conducting *tenkin* was employees' human resource development, followed by employees' treatment and appropriate deployment, results of personnel rotations for organizational management, vitalization of organizations and stimulation of employees, labor supply for business expansion and new branches, and selection and training of managers (JILPT 2017: 5). The number of the firms conducting *tenkin* grew according to the number of sites that these firms had. That is to say, the larger a company became, the more regular employees it had and the more branches it had, and then the more commonly it conducted *tenkin* (JILPT 2017: 5). The study illuminated that *tenkin* served as an iconic practice for a regular worker who belonged to a large company.

JILPT's study (2017) also displayed the gendered feature of *tenkin*. The rate of men who have experienced *tenkin* is proportionally higher than that of women (JILPT 2017: 6). Some individual workers, 11.6 percent of male workers and 14.6 percent of female workers, had asked for consideration [*hairyo*] from their employers, not to be transferred. The reasons for the request for the consideration were all related to their family as follows: for their parents' care, for children's education, and for childbearing and rearing, as their necessities were stipulated in Article 26 of the revised Child and Family Care Leave Law (MHLW 2010). They were followed by for marriage, for home ownership, and for spouses' work. Moreover, for all of the top three reasons, more men than women had requested exemptions [*menjo*] from the requirement of *tenkin*. These contemporary workers seemed to prioritize balancing their work and life over simply subjugating themselves to their employers. From the managements' point of view, too, 18.2 percent think that such requests for exemptions from male workers had increased in the last three years (JILPT 2017). The proportion declined to 11.7 percent for female workers, but these data showed that the practices of consideration and exemption regarding *tenkin* do take place in contemporary Japanese workplaces. With this data, in hand, the governmental committee (MHLW 2017a) advised Japanese firms to reorganize their practice of *tenkin*, so that workers with family responsibility could balance their *tenkin* and family lives. From the 2017 JILPT research and subsequent statement by the committee, we learn that some employees are no longer taking *tenkin* orders for granted, and their ways of thinking about their working lives and family lives are changing.

Nowadays the increasing numbers of women are playing pivotal roles at workplaces and the number of dual-income and dual-career couples is rising (Gender Equality Bureau 2023: 4). Embracing well-being in different ways from the conventional breadwinner relationship, women work hard to manage their careers and family relationship (Roberts 2011). More and more men are trying to commit to child-caring roles (Ishii-Kunz 2003; North 2014; Nakazato 2017). They are motivated not only by necessity, for example, when their wives have full-time jobs and they have no one else to take care of their children, but rather by a willingness to spend more time with their children and not solely be financial providers. Indeed, younger generations indicate more diverse views regarding getting married and having children, while having careers (Mirza 2016; Roberts 2016). The most recent study furthermore argues that younger generations have different views toward their lifestyles when compared with workers from the *Shōwa* era (Klien 2021).

Thus, people's attitudes toward family and work are becoming different and diverse in comparison to the former generation (Roberts 2014; Mathews 2014).

Nonetheless, the political and corporate attempts have been weak to integrate these new actors into the practice of *tenkin*. Various government policies and campaigns have only aimed to utilize female employees under the current structure. In 2016, the Act on the Promotion of Women's Active Engagement in Professional Life [*Josei katsuyaku suishin hō*] was enacted and companies with 301 employees and more are obliged to publish their action plans to promote their female employees (MHLW 2016). Since 2022, moreover, companies with less than 300 employees over 101 have become the subjects, too, and the obligation has included disclosure of various data of their company's gender-unequal situations (MHLW 2022). Yet, the market as well as the government have made few efforts to look into the fundamental issues underlying the practice of *tenkin*. As a result, women's economic participation and opportunity are very low as the Global Gender Gap Index indicates Japan's rank as 125th out of 146 countries (WEF 2023). If we see the index of "Legislators, senior officials, and managers," the rank goes down further to the 133rd (WEF 2023: 217). This means that among the world's 146 countries, the number of women who are in managerial positions is at the lowest level. Furthermore, the later quantitative research uncovered that the gender differences in the experiences of *tenkin* end up in gender pay gap of the workers in the same category (Sato, Hashimoto, and Owan 2019).

Recently the government has called for a "*Reiwa* Model" (Gender Equality Bureau 2023). They now specify the male-breadwinner and female-homemaker model as an outdated "*Shōwa* Model," which attributes its ground to the gender division of labor and produces the practice of long working hours. This has hindered workers who have limitations in hours and locations, mostly women due to their domestic responsibilities, from fulfilling their jobs and careers. The *Reiwa* Model will enable people who wish to work to engage more in their workplace while balancing their work and family lives, the government stipulates (Gender Equality Bureau 2023). In other words, the dual-career model is more and more promoted.

Under these dynamics, I determined to investigate Japanese firms' implementation of *tenkin* and the realities of the lives of dual-career families who experienced the practice of *tenkin*. I ask, how is *tenkin* produced? How do firms deal with transferred employees? If there are any practices in both workplace and home that individual workers play, what are they and what consciousness do the actors have of these practices? Then, what outcomes do their actions bring about? Finally, how should *tenkin* evolve?

Social Structure and Agency

The conceptual framework of structure and agency is the best fit to deliberate these research questions. I particularly rely on the views developed by Giddens, Bourdieu, and Ortner for an analytical framework of my ethnographic research, in analyzing processes of both corporate practices in conducting *tenkin* and workers' practices in acting toward *tenkin* in workplaces and homes, respectively.

Anthony Giddens (1979), one of the initial theorists who attempted to elucidate the relation between human beings' consciousness and actions and their social structure, discusses the "duality of structure" (Giddens 1979: 69) in *Central Problems in Social Theory: Action, Structure and Contradiction in Social Analysis*. Structures are both constraining and enabling and both means and outcomes. He sees them as having "transformative capacity" (Giddens 1979: 59–95). In the structure, actors realize their actions by reflexively monitoring what and how to act routinely and chronically, as well as by interacting with others in the society. With this "practical consciousness" (Giddens 1979: 24), the actors come to articulate their intentions, even if they can only offer a fragmentary account. In this sense, social actors are knowledgeable, and through practices conducted across time, they become able to choose and make decisions on their own. They are not unconscious but influence their structure. His view, thus, sheds light on human capabilities, or agency, within their social structures, although his theory barely explains how exactly the structure is transformed, as William H. Sewell Jr. (1992) pointed out.

Pierre Bourdieu's theory of practice provides more detailed elucidations on the relation between human beings' actions and their social structures. Bourdieu (1977), in his pioneering work, *Outline of a Theory of Practice*, elaborates on forms of human actions, or practices, which are influenced by their social structure and which in turn affect the reproduction of the structure. He calls the forms *habitus* (Bourdieu 1977), referring to human dispositions that are "collectively orchestrated without being the product of the orchestrating action of a conductor" (Bourdieu 1977: 72). To put it differently, in a certain structure, human beings do not simply follow rules. They are neither completely organized by others, nor are they fully controlled by their clear purposes of making actions. In certain structures, in which the actors share common sense or taken-for-granted understanding through history, they produce and reproduce their practices, controlled by the regularities of the group, while also expressing diverse dispositions in their social trajectories and positions. Because the members of the group belong to other different groups, too, the common sense or the taken-for-granted pervades the others across time and space, as Bourdieu describes *habitus* as "durable and transposable" (Bourdieu 1977: 72). In this way, the individual and collective practices are reproduced in the social structure. By *habitus*, people are not only constrained by their structure but also reconstructing the structure. In his *Masculine Domination* (2001), Bourdieu discusses, in relation to gender, how male-dominated social structure produces and reproduces *habitus* across time. Although it is implied that change can occur when dominant mechanisms and institutions are transformed by people's changing dispositions (Bourdieu 2001: 82–8), in the Kabyle society that he studied, common sense on gender helps to sustain male dominance.

Sherry Ortner, in her 1984 article, referring to Marshall Sahlins' theory of reproduction and transformation (1981), argues that change is brought about not by replacement of groups with alternative visions of the world, or revolution in Marx's meaning, but through human beings' attempts to apply traditional interpretations and practices into interactions with people from outside the society to build new relationships with the outsiders. Then they brought the new relationships to insiders, where the traditional relationships were influenced (Ortner 1984: 156). In short, when meanings of people's relationships change across space and time, their society may change.

Yet, this view requires more detailed accounts of consciousness and actions of human beings, as Ortner argues (1984, 2006). In other words, what drives people to adapt themselves to and embody new practices, rather than succumb to the conventional practices, in their relationships with others, needs to be explained. Ortner (1984, 2006) answers this question as follows: Human beings who have different interests in different social positions have "images and ideals of what constitutes goodness—in people, in relationships, and in conditions of life" (Ortner 1984: 152). So, they "seek to enhance their respective positions when opportunities arise, although they do so by means traditionally available to people in their positions" (Ortner 1984: 155). However, when the "traditional strategies are deployed in relation to novel phenomena which do not respond to those strategies in traditional ways, change comes about" (Ortner 1984: 155). From Ortner's (1984) viewpoint, people themselves who inherently sought better lives individually as well as collectively have capabilities for transformation.

These conceptions of inherit capability and collectivity of human actions are further discussed in her later book, *Anthropology and Social Theory: Culture, Power, and the Acting Subject* (Ortner 2006). First, Ortner calls such actions by individuals "agency in the pursuit and enactment of projects," meaning "local logics of the good and the desirable and how to pursue them" (Ortner 2006: 145). For Ortner, agency is not only invoked under domination and resistance, which she calls as "agency as exercise of or against power" (Ortner 2006: 139). Human beings, who are inherently motivated to seek the better in their everyday living, shape desires and strive for intentions according to culturally constituted repertoires in diverse ways. Their "projects are full-blown 'serious games,' involving the intense play of multiply positioned subjects pursuing cultural goals within a matrix of local inequalities and power differentials" (Ortner 2006: 144). In their projects, while they interact with others from different structures and make new relationships with them, they may change the meanings of their conventional practices and adapt themselves to new practices that grow out of their own structures of life (Ortner 2006: 146–47). Since people live across multiple structures, such as employment and family structures, as well as those in other regions and nations, their new actions can influence other people through interactions, and further transpose the meanings of these other people's conventional practices. When the new groups embodying new practices become mainstream, the structures are transformed.

With these conceptual frameworks of agency and structural transformation, I posed the following more detailed questions in my qualitative research to explore individual workers' attitudes toward *tenkin* in contemporary employment and family realms: what are the desires, intentions, and subsequent actions of the workers in their experience of *tenkin*? How do they negotiate in their own minds and with others? What kinds of relationships in their workplaces and homes constrain and enable the actors to reproduce or transform their practices in *tenkin* itself as well as *tenkin*-related lives? Do these negotiations bring about better situations and better lives for the workers in the workplaces and homes? If so or not, how and why? This research provides the detailed accounts of how the workers manage their careers and whether their actions make changes to their work and family spheres.

The Internal Labor Market as Economic Ground for *Tenkin*

Among the umbrella questions I noted above, the first one—the production of *tenkin*—can be answered by existing literature. First and foremost, *tenkin* is ascribed to the establishment of the "Internal Labor Market" (Doeringer and Piore 1971) in the 1950s. The postwar Japanese economy was booming and the labor market was expanding (Sugayama 2011). In the labor market, *tenkin* became taken for granted as an economically rationale practice for regularly hired male workers. At the same time, the "housewifization" of Japanese women was promoted (Ochiai 1994).

The Internal Labor Market, hereafter ILM, is "an administrative unit, such as a manufacturing plant, within which the pricing and allocation of labor is governed by a set of administrative rules and procedures" (Doeringer and Piore 1971: 2). Distinguished from an external labor market of the conventional economic theory where pricing, allocating, as well as training decisions are controlled directly by economic variables, the administrative rules and procedures of the ILM accord certain rights and privileges to the internal labor force, for example, by filling jobs from within the firm and protecting their employment continuity, even at entry ports, from direct competition by other workers in the external labor market (Doeringer and Piore 1971: 2).

Three major factors: skill specificity, on-the-job training, and customary law are responsible for the existence and determination of the administrative rules of the ILM (Doeringer and Piore 1971: 13–27). Skill specificity, or job or technology specificity, enables workers to anticipate trouble, diagnose its source, and minimize equipment downtime in their daily work and thereby cut the cost and improve efficiency. On-the-job training, or informal training at the production lines, enables both trainers and trainees to learn specific skills and produce products while to avoid reducing the number of workers for formal costly training programs. Customary law or custom at the workplace, means "an unwritten set of rules based largely upon past practice or precedent" (Doeringer and Piore 1971: 23). When the preceding two factors are developed in a work group, employment becomes more stable and the same workers come into regular and repeated contact with each other and generate and experience unwritten rules. The process increasingly makes the market internalized and less responsive to dynamic economic forces in the external labor market, as occurred in American industrial history (Doeringer and Piore 1971: 13–40).

Once the ILM is established, three characteristics accrue: closed ports of entry and exit; a broad range of mobility clusters; and rigid rules for mobility (Doeringer and Piore 1971: 41–63). All three function as an allocative structure of the market and therefore determine its existence. With these characteristics of the allocative structures of the ILM, workers tend to be hired into a single, often low-skilled entry job classification, and vertically and horizontally transferred internally within mobility clusters "the grouping of jobs within which an employee is customarily upgraded, downgraded, transferred, and laid off" (Doeringer and Piore 1971: 50), according to rules that often depend upon ability and seniority in the market and determine priority and ranking of the mobility. This structure is efficient for both employers and employees because the workers' firm-specific skill development under the desired long-term employment helps the former reduce personnel costs and the latter secure their jobs even in economic fluctuations caused by economic downturn or technological change (Doeringer and Piore 1971: 41–63).

In Japan, records from the *Edo* period (Shimpo and Saitō 1989; Saitō 2002, 2006) indicate the existence of the ILM. White-collar workers had wide mobility and the distinctive features of the ports of entry. By the end of the 1870s in the *Meiji* era, the ILM appeared to be settled for white-collar workers in large firms. While the state was increasingly modernized, white-collar workers tended to experience various positions in different sections within their company to expand their business as well as to attain top or middle managerial positions (Morikawa 1981). Yet, ports of entry for white-collar workers were not rigid in the government-owned Yawata Steel Works, for example, and most workers' skills were developed through job hopping in the external labor market (Sugayama 2011). It was the postwar era that workers' long-term employment security was developed and the ILM was established in Japan. Accordingly, *tenkin* for white-collar workers was installed as a purposeful practice for workers as well as for their employers.

Beyond Doeringer and Piore's (1971) theory of allocative structures, relocation for white-collar workers occurs not only by closing plants, or offices, but also by their personnel assignments during their careers, as documented by the anthropologist, Thomas Rohlen (1974). In his study of a Japanese bank in the late 1960s, Rohlen reported that the bank conducted relocation as an alternative to dismissal if it evaluated workers as incompetent in their assessments (Rohlen 1974: 80). Although there was an obvious cost in retaining people who did not contribute, were potentially disruptive, or had lethargy bred by an over-dependence on the company, the bank almost never attempted to implement dismissal as they believed that it would destroy morale and activate the company union (Rohlen 1974). The relocations were conducted regularly every fall at the same time as promotions (Rohlen 1974: 136). The bank not only preferred not to dismiss employees, but also avoided having to demote them. However, if the latter was called for, in an attempt to preserve the worker's dignity and status, he was not overtly demoted in rank, but rather transferred to smaller, less important offices in more rural areas in which his prestige and authority dropped with a reduction of his duties (Rohlen 1974: 148–49), which may have helped to "defer the public identification of losers in the hierarchical organization" (Hatveny and Pucik 1981: 476). If the person was evaluated as less competent, he would spend his entire career moving from his position to other small posts, never moving back to more glamorous and more challenging work of the main office (Rohlen 1974: 149). In this system of shuffling the workers judged incompetent or undesirable, the possibilities of relocation lasted throughout their career, including reemployment by the subsidiaries (Rohlen 1974: 76), which can be interpreted as reassignment [*tenseki*]. This practice of relocation, according to Rohlen (1974: 149), further motivated the bank's younger workers by opening up room for them to rise, which enhanced their engagement and commitment to their bank.

Rohlen may have overemphasized the advantageous aspects of the relocations for both employers and employees. There have been lawsuits filed over relocations that functioned as harassment. In the Tonami Transport Service Case, for example, a whistle-blowing employee was transferred from the Toyama head office to a Tokyo office after he leaked the existence of a cartel his firm had made with other companies (MHLW 2015). Soon after, when the Tokyo office was closed, he was transferred back to an office in Toyama that dealt with education, but to a seat secluded from other workers. He was given no work, nor promotions for approximately two decades. The court recognized the man's claim and ruled that the firm was liable to pay damages for harassment (MHLW 2015). Since relocation is the prerogative of employers, it is likely to be manipulated this way.

Relocation as the alternative to dismissal for white-collar workers continued throughout the 1990s to the beginning of the 2000s, during which the relocation for blue-collar workers faded away. There was high intra-firm mobility, including interregional movement, which caused a lot of *tanshin funin*[1] (Rebick 2005: 32).

Among all the purposes of the practice of *tenkin*, job rotation is often described as fundamentally important for white-collar workers to acquire firm-specific managerial skills. According to Pucik (1984), once hired right after graduation of higher educational institutions, white-collar employees had initial training in a position to which they were assigned according to their firm's business needs at the time, their personal preferences, and assessment of their skills, and in which they were expected to familiarize themselves with their firm as well as to acquire basic skills. The experience generally determined their "functional specialty" (Pucik 1984), within which they were transferred from one section to another.

The frequency of the rotation depended on a worker's specialty and existence of vacancies. The increase in corporate spin-offs may have resulted in loans to subsidiaries, though this did not necessarily cause downward mobility, but only led to a change of their "field" (Pucik 1984: 267) from the larger point of view. For instance, some companies transferred seasoned managers to other group companies, to instill their managerial skills in the group (Hatvany and Pucik 1981: 475). Through all these cycles of job rotations, they were expected to develop their skills to become future managers in their organizations, or "generalists within specialties who know how to handle uncertain situations in their business" (Koike 1991: 14–19, 1997: 43–50). This practice of job rotation can be interpreted as mobility within clusters according to the rules, which are the key factors in the allocation of labor in the ILM (Doeringer and Piore 1971). Thus, intra-firm mobility as job rotation is regarded as taken-for-granted for white-collar workers' employment, even if it may result in a sudden move of a residence [*tenkin*].

Associated with the practices above such as relocation and job rotation, seniority-based in-house promotion is common among white-collar workers. When promoted, *tenkin* seems to be carried out, but is fraught with uncertainty for workers on most occasions. Throughout their working lives, the workers Pucik studied were "granted annual seniority pay increases, in addition to salary increase based on merit" (Pucik 1984: 259). For those workers, promotion in ranks, job titles, or positions (Pucik 1984: 260) was ambitiously sought in the hierarchical ladder, because it was a competition with others in the peer group to get to the position as fast as possible (Pucik 1984: 270; Rohlen 1974: 135–48). Rosenbaum (1979) called this a "tournament." Those who won the competitions may have experienced *tenkin* if the positions were located far away from their domicile, even if the workers' ranks did not change.

Yet, the competitions were held within certain conditions, such as within a certain range of ages, length of service, and the number of vacancies to fill (Rohlen 1974: 135–48). This is firstly because positions to be offered were often limited and varied each year because, under the long-term employment system, they were opened solely through the combination of promotion, retirement, reorganization, and expansion (Rohlen 1974: 136). Secondly, the whole promotion system was the embodiment of the cultural values of persistent, dependable, careful work, and most importantly, harmony, all of which, and the last the most, were evaluated as crucial for promotion (Rohlen 1974: 144–45). The emphasis on competition relying on these cultural factors may have developed critical administrative rules of upward mobility involving *tenkin*, and may have stimulated the workers and embedded the practice more in the employment system.

Under the unspoken rules, *tenkin* is conducted within the disguise of the promotion process. Employees were transferred to other departments or companies, not clearly knowing what the transfer meant, because their personnel department and managers hardly gave any feedback regarding their appraisal results (Pucik 1984: 269–70). Nonetheless, this ambiguous evaluating process was sustained in the workplaces, as it not only prevented the workers from feeling that they were in the "bottom line" (Pucik 1984: 270) of the hierarchy but also helped them to acquire different skills and "find a niche in the organization for which they were especially well suited" (Hatvany and Pucik 1981: 475). In other words, through rotation and indirect feedback, employees are strung along by employers and kept motivated to work harder for the next probable promotion, even though it may not happen. This coincides with *tenkin* as relocation for long-term employment security, and most importantly, indicates how each firm's practice of *tenkin* has been developed as a package. Even if the true nature is not clearly visible, understanding of it is certainly manifest in the commitment of the actors in white-collar employment in Japan.

In blue-collar employment, too, *tenkin* was conducted, but it was not as common as in while-collar employment. In the postwar late 1940s, after winning battles for employment protection from employers, in Toshiba, for example (Gordon 1985), many of blue-collar workers began to receive intra-firm mobility, including *tenkin* in order to secure their jobs. Labor reorganization starting in the 1950s due to plant modernization and technological innovation also contributed to shifts in labor markets (Gordon 1985: 387). In the new factories of the process industry[2] that started operation in the Keihin area in 1960, for example, only 30 percent of the blue-collar workers were newly hired and almost all of the others were transferred from the other old plants of the company located in faraway cities (Yamamoto 1967). Following rapid economic growth in the 1950s, the process industries found themselves in a deeper predicament, because technological progress arising during the period required scrapping and building of their plants and thereby the employees in original plants with old skills were subject to losing their jobs and also had difficulty in finding new jobs within the industry (Yamamoto 1967: 93–94). With serious labor disputes still occurring and probable suspension of operation in mind, the employers decided to relocate and secure the workers, rather than to dismiss them, and attempted to avoid possible loss of anticipated profit (Yamamoto 1967: 268–70). Also, since the periodic recruiting system for new school graduates was settled by around this time, the employers may also have contemplated probable difficulty in hiring skilled workers when they were necessary. From employees' point of view, accepting the relocation outweighed their reluctance to change their domiciles, knowing that this was the only way to retain their jobs (Yamamoto 1967: 94). These records imply that the shift of the labor markets for blue-collar workers were brought about by deliberate and rational decisions based on efficiency that employers made at the time, as discussed in Doeringer and Piore's (1971) theory of the ILM. Moreover, such decisions were conducive to their employees, too, during the time of economic fluctuation. In this way, blue-collar workers were assured the "same status as the white-collars" (Dore 1973) or "full membership" (Gordon 1985) as regular employees of the firms. They were rarely targeted for dismissal in economic declines or because of technological developments. This shift of labor relations, associated with closed ports of entry, wider mobility clusters, and rigid rules for mobility, all in all contributed to the development of the ILM and the practice of *tenkin*, while, women continued to be excluded from these practices (Roberts 1994).

Yet, sooner or later, correlated with further weakening of company unions, increased non-regular full-time and part-time workers, and production shifts overseas, the practices of relocation including *tenkin* for the blue-collar workers have become less common. This may have influenced my snowball sample, in which I could barely find any blue-collar workers who had experienced *tenkin* as dual-income couples. Consequently, I am not including blue-collar *tenkin* in my empirical research, although it is an important fact that *tenkin* was conducted for blue-collar workers when Japan's postwar economy was growing.

Japanese Employment Structures Compatible to *Tenkin*

Here, some may wonder why Japanese white-collar workers are the subjects of *tenkin*, establishing the ILM. In their theory based on the research in the United States, Doeringer and Piore (1971) say the Internal Labor Market most often existed in blue-collar employment. They describe white-collar managerial workers as job-hoppers in the external labor market who seek to utilize their universal skills to manage people.

There are two answers to the question: customs and gendered social structure. First, the establishment and development of the ILM including the practice of *tenkin* for white-collar workers in Japan is strongly related to certain cultural norms. In a corporate hierarchical system, Japanese white-collar workers are more prone to see *tenkin* as necessary to achieve various purposes. Labor Law scholar, Hirokuni Tabata (1998), provides another insight that explains a rationale of the workers' attitudes in the ILM. He argues that Japanese employment, often described as a firm-community, or a community as a firm, enables efficiency as well. When a firm operates like a community, it helps workers seek common interests for all members, including shareholders and managers. Long-term employment increases the competitiveness and profit of firms vis-à-vis other companies in the market. In this way, the firm-community comes into operation as an "interest community," which reinforces the workers' incentive to work for the preservation of their organizations and inspires unions' cooperative attitudes. Meanwhile, the seniority-based merit system also stimulates the workers to compete with other members within the firm. The system primarily determines the workers' wages according to age and length of service, with fine adjustments based on appraisals of their performances and abilities (Tabata 1998: 211). This economic individualism enhances efficiency both in the firm and the Internal Labor Market. The functions of the efficient firm-community should help to explain the economic and cultural inducement of Japanese white-collar (male) workers' long-term commitment and strong engagement with their firms. The workers who are thus socialized in a certain frame and simultaneously constitute their own identity make all the diverse practices of *tenkin* indispensable, while helping the practices establish and develop as pivotal rules of the allocative structures of the ILM. Under this norm, even if some male workers try to avoid *tenkin* due to difficulties in managing their family lives and bring lawsuits against their employers, the courts make decisions in favor of the companies, taking their business needs into consideration (Hamaguchi 2011).

In fact, there have been a few lawsuits in which men in dual-career couples sought nullification of their *tenkin* orders. These help us understand the difficulties workers face in defying the practice of *tenkin*. In the 1986 TOA

Paint Case, for example, an employee of the company, who had an elderly mother, a working wife, and a two-year-old child, sought to have the court nullify the dismissal that he suffered due to his rejection of a *tenkin* order (Hamaguchi 2011). The employee, who had been ordered to do *tenkin* from Kobe city to Hiroshima city, rejected the order. The company then decided to send another person from Nagoya city to Hiroshima city, but this, in turn, required them to fill in the vacant post in Nagoya. The man was thereby ordered to go to Nagoya, but he rejected the order again for the care of his mother and child. Finally, the company forced the appointment on him, and when he refused again, he was dismissed, on the grounds that his continued rejection of *tenkin* violated company work rules stipulating that the firm can order *tenkin* as required for business reasons. The Supreme Court decided that the company's *tenkin* order and dismissal notice were both valid. In its decision, the court said that disadvantages in family lives caused by *tenkin* were normal inconveniences, which employees should accept and endure (Hamaguchi 2011). Since this time, over three decades, this Supreme Court ruling has been used as a judicial precedent. In another case, the 1996 Teikoku Hormone Manufacturing Case, when nullification of the *tenkin* order was sought, the court decided in favor of the company, referring to the previous case, and supported the verification of the *tenkin* order (Hamaguchi 2011).

According to labor law scholar Takashi Araki (2011: 7–9), in lawsuits that challenge the validity of transfer orders, the courts ought to consider two perspectives: contractual grounds and abuse of the right to issue orders. Under the Japanese long-term employment system, flexible deployment of regular employees through transfers is one of the measures employers can use to compensate for the lack of flexibility in firing and hiring during economic fluctuations. This gives employers a certain discretionary authority, free from judicial control. They can establish their right to order transfers, including *tenkin*, by prescribing in their work rules book [*shūgyō kisoku*][3] that such occasions may happen out of business necessity. In lawsuits, the courts have examined the validity of transfers in light of stipulations, such as whether employers may have restricted workers' places of work. On the other hand, in the process of the examination, the courts have also considered whether transfers cause inconveniences to workers and their families. In other words, they have considered whether transfers are an abuse of rights. But, as Araki (2011) discusses, the courts, including the Supreme Court, are generally reluctant to nullify transfer orders and make decisions in favor of plaintiffs, or workers, interpreting the term "business necessity" broadly. For example, the interpretation includes appropriate allocation of the workforce, improvement of business efficiency, development of workers' abilities, and enhancement of morale and harmonious administration of the business (Araki 2011: 9). In court, firms always have the advantage, and this has allowed them to maintain the legitimacy of the practice of *tenkin*.

More recently, some lower courts have tended to take family problems into consideration and issued decisions that nullify *tenkin* orders. In the Meijitosho Publishing Case in 2002, the Tokyo District Court recognized the abuse of rights in the *tenkin* order for a male employee. His wife had a job, and they had two children with atopic dermatitis, as well as parents who would be in need of elder care in the future (Hamaguchi 2011). This time, the court mentioned Article 26 (Consideration [*hairyo*] of *Tenkin*) in the Child and Family Care Leave Law (revised in 2001) which stipulates that the employer must consider whether *tenkin* will cause the employee difficulties in childcare or elder care (Hamaguchi 2011). But, the case also lays bare that the male worker is indeed ordered to do *tenkin* even though he asks his company to consider his private situation. Faced with a *tenkin* order, these workers' bargaining power seems to be weak. Why? In addition to the previous lost cases in courts that may have made them think they can do nothing, there may also be a fear of "retaliation" [*hōfuku*], as actually seen in a practice of Toyota (Tsuji 2011: 375), in which transfers to unimportant posts were used as harassment. This was also mentioned in the Tonami Transport Service Case above. Even if employers allow their employees to raise family situations and attempt to take them sympathetically into account in their personnel decisions, the employers may also force the workers to assent to a promotion delay or bad appraisal result (Kumazawa 1989, 59), which means losing their place in their peer group in the corporate hierarchy. Company unions are weak, too, primarily because they themselves agreed to accept the practice as an alternative to dismissal, as I described earlier, and also because they have strong interests in cooperating with their firms to maintain the employers' initiatives to include them and exclude the other non-union members (Kumazawa 1989; Gordon 2012). These practices are taken for granted, also because workers may have an obscure sense of the meaning of a job, as Robert Cole's (1979) put it in the 1970s. From his comparative study on workers in the United States and Japan, Cole argued as follows:

> The job a Japanese employee reports that he is performing may actually stand for a whole range of jobs that he is carrying out. That is, when a Japanese respondent reports that he is, say, a driller, he will be using it as a generic term to span a whole range of activities carried out by drillers in his section, activities which an American worker would be likely to perceive as separate jobs, and thus would be more likely to list in his job history report. In short, the relative lack of sharp jurisdictional definitions of job duties on the part of both management and workers tends to make Japanese workers less conscious of job changes. Thus it is not simply a matter of underreporting, but rather that the very

concept of job and job change seems to differ in the two societies (The U.S. and Japan). (Cole 1979: 99–100)

This suggests that the Japanese white-collar workers in his study have wider mobility clusters (Doeringer and Piore 1971) within which to be transferred, perhaps not only laterally but also vertically, and furthermore, this is ruled by custom. The vague sense of a job shared by the workers possibly in turn influenced the administrative rules of the markets in a way to make people assume the mobility, perhaps including *tenkin*, as taken-for-granted. The roles of customs are crucial here again for excluding those who are not "us," and thereby discriminating against them. All in all, in a corporate-oriented society like Japan, workers are vulnerable to the interests that their firms pursue. The pursuit of the economic efficiency and dependence on custom have thus gone hand-in-hand and therefore a few workers who are reluctant to cooperate and commit to their firms have no choice but to accept the practice.

Tenkin and the Gender Division of Labor

The second, more critical and fundamental reason why Japanese white-collar workers are the subjects of *tenkin* and the ILM, I argue, is that the whole social structure sustaining their employment rests on the gender division of labor. In other words, ILM practices, including *tenkin*, for Japanese white-collar employees rest on the male-breadwinner and female-homemaker model that has distinctly sustained the whole Japanese socio-economic system throughout the postwar period, as Mari Ōsawa (1993) lays out.

To begin with, it was not until the end of the twentieth century that female workers became the subjects of *tenkin*. This was primarily because they were rarely seen as members of the ILM, as Alice Lam (1992) argues. According to Lam, the mechanism of the ILM itself functions as a structural source of labor market inequality and perpetuates discrimination, in the very way that it preserves the rights and privileges of those currently employed. In other words, the set of rules of the ILM in Japanese firms is more exclusive and discriminatory toward outsiders than that in the Western firms that Doeringer and Piore analyzed (Lam 1992: 27). Lam attributed the fundamental cause for this to the nature of the rules and practices governing the Japanese ILM, which are based more on personal characteristics than job classifications (Lam 1992: 28). This perspective resonates with the argument by Robert Cole (1979) earlier.

Moreover, from the feminist perspective, since the exclusion of women goes hand-in-hand with job segregation in capitalist societies that maintains the superiority of men over women in both public and private spheres (Ueno 2009), this mechanism will reproduce itself. This is how institutions with the ILMs automatically remain male-oriented and women are kept excluded (Lam 1992: 33–44). Vera Mackie (2002) further discusses that this marginalization takes place not only in the workplace but also in the whole society, in which the archetypal citizen in the political system is a male, heterosexual, able-bodied, fertile, white-collar worker.

Therefore, even though most female white-collar clerical workers held regular jobs and played important roles in their offices (Ogasawara 1998), it was expected that employment only lasted until they married. Though some blue-collar regular employees took full responsibility in production lines (Roberts 1994), they were vulnerable to managerial decisions to transfer their jobs to production sites overseas (Roberts 2014). In the 2000s, the rate of women's non-regular employment has risen (Gordon 2012). This means that an increasing number of female workers were thrown permanently into the external labor market. There, they had few chances for skill development, career development, promotion, or long-term employment, which are the fundamental reasons for *tenkin* in Japan's ILM.

With the enactment of the Equal Employment Opportunity Law in 1986, the course-based hiring system was installed and some of the large Japanese corporations hired some women, if not many, as white-collar career-track [*sōgōshoku*] workers (Lam 1992, 1993). They also offered a conversion system to women who had worked as clerical non-career-track [*ippannshoku*] employees, which allowed them a chance to change their employment category to a managerial career track (Lam 1993).

But very few female employees newly hired in such career-track positions were granted opportunities for training and promotion equally with male counterparts unless they were able to conform to the male-dominated organizational rules and practices. In the conversion system, too, because they had been given fewer chances of job rotation for training while they held clerical jobs, their experience could not be evaluated highly enough to compete with their male colleagues on an equal basis, resulting in few women utilizing the system (Lam 1993). Consequently, women lacked the skills and networks indispensable to win the career tournament and climb up the hierarchal ladder. Their contributions were restricted to mundane jobs and made the personnel division or their bosses think that they are not ready to be in a senior position (Yashiro 1995, 99). As a result, the career-track positions remained widely occupied by male white-collar workers (Lam 1992, 1993; Yashiro 1995; Senda and Ōuchi 2002), and this vicious circle of discrimination against women surely seemed to affect the few descriptions of female workers' experience of *tenkin*.

Occasionally, even though women were given opportunities of *tenkin*, many of them in fact had difficulty in accepting them. This resulted not only in thrusting these women workers into the external labor market but also in further reinforcing the gender division in their workplaces. In a general merchandise store, for instance, female regular full-time employees chose to work part-time when the store adopted a new personnel management system in the 2000s. This system differentiated the types of workers based on whether or not they could accept *tenkin* (Kim 2008). Though they took an equal share of core responsibilities in the store, they were classified as part-timers which denied them chances for promotion. They fell into this category because they did not want to be transferred to other stores. Dividing the types of workers by *tenkin* decreased the number of female employees who were actually unable to fulfill the requirement as well as those who were not confident to do so because of an increasing negative feeling about *tenkin* (Kim 2008). In the end, the difference in treatment reinforced depressed aspirations in younger women workers and made them abandon their desires for upward mobility, as sociologist Nemoto Kumiko (2016) has argued.

These gendered outcomes involving *tenkin* were replicated in public schools, where teachers of both genders were required to play the same roles in the workplaces. Blaine P. Connor (2010) studied on the transfer of public school teachers in Nagasaki Prefecture in his Ph.D. dissertation and found that only female teachers opted out after they experienced a series of mandatory *tenkin*. In attempting to fulfill the transfer requirement, which was established to redress the imbalance in personnel between the outer and main islands of Nagasaki Prefecture in accordance with nationwide educational recentralization, the women soon felt difficulties in balancing their roles in both work and family. Unions tried to do away with the system, however, the system met needs for other teachers who wanted to move away from peripheral areas. In addition, some teachers were satisfied that their professional ideals could be developed through transfers. They felt "pride, pleasure, self-worth, and legitimate authority over parents and students" (Connor 2010, 335) as prefectural public servants. Thus, embraced by the actors themselves, transfers for Nagasaki teachers were settled as a practice, based on the gender division of labor model (Connor 2010).

In this way, women have faced structural discrimination whenever they encountered any of the various forms of *tenkin* in their workplaces. They have not been seen as subjects who can accept and fulfill responsibility at *tenkin*. Even if they are given chances of *tenkin*, they end up in taking "exit options" (Schoppa 2006) from pursuing their careers due to the difficulty in balancing their work and life. This has resulted in few women desiring or achieving mobility to managerial positions through *tenkin*, which helps the structure reproduce itself.

Tenkin in Family Lives

Furthermore, without doubt, such structural constraints reach the family lives of women, if they are married. When they confront their husband's *tenkin*, they are primarily and always expected to take secondary roles for all family members in the practice of *tenkin*. In many modernized societies, family issues are women's issues. Japan is not an exception, as many social scientists have reported (Lebra 1984; Rosenberger 2001; Goldstein-Gidoni 2012; Vogel 2013). It has been always women, or more precisely housewives, who are primarily responsible for reproductive roles at home. Only recently did some studies start paying attention to men, particularly their roles in childcare and partial participation in housework, although these remained supporting roles (Ishii-Kunz 1995, 2003; North 2014).

In the case of *tenkin*, too, women have been primarily described as having the role of handling family issues. As wives and mothers, they have been thrust into difficulties caused by sudden inter-regional transfers of their corporate husbands (Tanaka 1991, 2002; Kurotani 2005). Yet, there are also some men who seem to be constrained in family lives because of *tenkin*. Some recent lawsuits illustrate these men's struggles at home as husbands and fathers (Hamaguchi 2011). Women and men are considered separately according to their roles so that I can tease out crucial factors here that have made *tenkin* more deeply embedded in Japanese society than elsewhere.

It was in the 1980s that *tenkin* caught public attention with respect to its influence on family lives. The term, *tanshin funin*, was increasingly featured in the media, which reported that it not only caused illness of the transferees but also affected their children's growth. According to Yūko Tanaka's (1991) study of *tanshin funin*, it used to be that *tenkin* was often experienced by managers who sought promotion. They were accompanied by all the family members, including younger school-age children. However, associated with the rise in the number of *tenkin* in the 1980s, the transferees and their families found it increasingly necessary to decide to live separately, in other words, to send the transferees alone, so that neither the children's education nor care for elderly parents would be disrupted. This resulted in *tanshin funin* for the transferees. When Tanaka conducted her study, one in five families made such decisions. Yet since 1984, when a murder-suicide occurred involving a mother who killed her child and then killed herself while her husband lived separately due to *tanshin funin*, this kind of family formation has been raised as a social problem (Tanaka 1991).

In the meantime, along with the dynamic shift of the Japanese firms' management due to the economic recession in the 1990s, a wider range of workers, including non-managerial workers and blue-collar workers, came to be involved in *tenkin*. Around this time, the average age of the wives of men undergoing *tenkin* was 33.6 years old (Tanaka 2002). This tendency helped direct more social attention to *tanshin funin* and the issues related to it, such as high levels of stress and mental problems among the transferees themselves, as well as their family members who had decided to live separately from their husbands and fathers (Tanaka 2002).

These issues accruing in families due to *tanshin funin* seemed to affect Japanese companies' attitudes toward their employees' decision making in *tenkin* and family lives. While acknowledging *tanshin funin* and providing related allowances, including housing support, they seemed to have recommended, or even coerced, the family of the transferees to move altogether. Noriko Okifuji's (1991) non-fictional book well documented how she and her husband were subjects of coercion. As a dual-career couple raising two children in Tokyo, they both had responsible white-collar jobs. Both of them were supportive of each other's careers. Then her husband received a *tenkin* order to go to Sapporo for promotion. He began to importune her to quit her job and move together with him to distant, snowy Hokkaido. He seemed to be pressured by his boss who said, "You are the kind of a man who cannot convince your wife [*nyōbō*][4] to follow!" (Okifuji 1991, 32). This Okifuji case clarified how gender roles embedded in the practice of *tenkin* force men to show commitment to their firms and act as breadwinners, while women take supporting roles as homemakers. Although the term, "follow" [*tsuiteiku*][5], reinforces an aesthetic image of a trailing spouse who prioritizes her husband in the case of *tenkin*, some women like Okifuji seem to be constrained by this norm, as was another woman in the book who also described the gender role expectations as the domination of a husband over a wife (Okifuji 1991).

The roles of wives were more vividly portrayed in cases of *tenkin* overseas. Anthropologist Sawa Kurotani (2005) studied Japanese corporate wives who were transferred with their husbands to the United States due to *tenkin*. According to Kurotani, most of the wives willingly followed others' expectations to follow their corporate husbands and maintain their "home away from home" in the United States. Their purpose was to enable the husbands to give full physical and mental commitment to their work. Although some of the wives who had careers of their own in Japan expressed resentment about these roles often forced on them by their husband's company, others accepted these primary roles for their family, seeing them as "work." But, while taking full responsibility at home overseas, some came to question and negotiate their domesticity. Influenced by other ways of living they went through in the United States, their "homemaking practices become more intentional, the everyday becomes not so everyday, and the mundane takes on a new significance" (Kurotani 2005, 219). Eventually, some wives came to see their domestic roles as problematic. This was unexpectedly different from their original ways of thinking, though most of them had to remain in their domestic sphere in the end. Here in Kurotani's book, the wives of the overseas corporate transferees had the same experience of fulfillment and constraint, which was conceptualized by sociologist Takie Sugiyama Lebra (1984). While *tenkin* appears to encourage women in playing domestic roles, it actually reinforces their structural constraints, as they themselves become aware across time.

Despite the constraints these women experienced due to *tenkin*, the clearcut gender division of labor in the practice of *tenkin* has made them feel that their experience is their domestic problem. In the home, it is always taken for granted that women are primarily responsible for family issues. There is no chance to negotiate. Okifuji (1991), too, had a series of arguments with her husband at home, however, she eventually abandoned her desire to continue her job, encountering her husband's insistence and social norms. Connor's (2010) study on Nagasaki public teachers above also suggested the women were constrained by their domestic roles as wives and mothers as well as by their public responsibility as workers. Women are thus structurally constrained in both public and domestic spheres through *tenkin*, and this is how the practice has been established, developed, and sustained.

Under this structure, which Chizuko Ueno calls "capitalism and patriarchy" (2009), women cannot be the primary actors in workplaces, nor secondary actors in families. Women are supposed to take care responsibility in the domestic sphere. It is now clear that, as Mari Ōsawa (1993) puts it, this very structure contributes to sustaining the corporate-oriented society by making both genders think this division of labor is beneficial, although some women and men both have come to question the system.

This clear-cut gender division of labor is obvious in men's experience of *tenkin*, too, though such descriptions in the literature are rare. But we have seen, for instance, how Okifuji's (1991) book depicted her husband's ambivalent experience, in which he had encouraged his wife's aspiration to keep her position of responsibility and resisted his co-workers' slanders against it, while he started to show strong frustration and resentment against his wife's attempts to send him alone to his *tenkin*. Required to experience *tenkin* in order to be promoted, and also suffering from difficulties in his everyday life in Sapporo, where his co-workers kept asking him why his wife did not follow, he ended up accepting the conventional notion that a wife should follow her husband on *tenkin* (Okifuji 1991). In Connor's (2010) cases of Nagasaki public teachers, again, although married men struggled with frequent *tenkin*, they made the conventional choice to accept the obligation for their own sake, to maintain self-worth and pride. Such attitudes of married men seem to have kept men's difficulties arising from *tenkin* under the surface.

Yet, as Hirokuni Tabata (1998) pinpoints in concluding his discussion of the efficient firm-community in future Japanese employment, the changing situations in the labor market along with economic globalization, including an increase in non-regular employment, frequent transfer and early retirement programs for regular workers, as well as gender bias in employment as a whole, may weaken the credibility of the firm-community in its protection, which "may strengthen the individualism of Japanese workers and help them create an alternative solidarity among workers, especially professional contractual workers" (Tabata 1998, 213). Indeed, the above-noted JILPT (2017) research indicated that the increasing number of Japanese workers are asking for exemption from *tenkin*. But is it going to be one of the triggers to transform the cultural, gendered employment system? Mari Ōsawa (1993) also argues, if married couples are more gender equal, in other words, if men do housework equally with women and women earn equally with men, it strengthens women's power in the corporate-oriented society. Sawa Kurotani (2005) predicts in the conclusion to her book that "as an expatriate Japanese husband and wife actively participate in each other's work, their conjugal relationship also begins to change into a more egalitarian partnership" (Kurotani 2005, 219). Are Japanese men and women increasingly going beyond the dominant gendered distinctions? If so, how?

METHODOLOGY

I employed diverse approaches. I aimed to understand not only the operations of the practices of *tenkin*, but also the people's consciousness, choices, and actions related to the practices in their relationships with bosses, subordinates, co-workers and friends, and family members in diverse settings. The main approach consisted of in-depth qualitative interviews with two main focus groups: Japanese firms and Japanese dual-career [*tomobataraki*] couples who conducted and experienced the practice of *tenkin*, respectively. They were seven large firms that were diverse in their industries, number of employees and locations, and forty-six Japanese married people, forty women and six men, who worked for firms located in Japan. Appendix A is a summary of the firms. For individual interviewees, refer to Appendix B. Throughout the interviews, I introduced myself not only as the doctoral researcher, but as the past career-track worker in a Japanese private company who had *tenkin* three times. By doing so, I showed both subjective and objective stances toward *tenkin* to my informants, and thereby, tried to elicit their honest accounts. In fact, once I introduced myself to them that way, they soon understood my purpose of the research and the interviews became interactive. The other approach consisted of participant observation in social events. As Emerson, Fretz, and Shaw (2001) put it, through the participant observation,

I inscribed the social discourse of *tenkin* on fieldnotes and explored its social settings of particular groups.

The Firms

Initially, in June 2015, I attempted to obtain access to Human Resources departments of approximately ten firms by sending request letters directly to them by post. I chose sixteen firms that had more than 1,000 employees and marked high sales records in the industry, according to the Corporate Quarterly Report for Recruitement published by Tōyō Keizai Shinpōsha (2014). The firms were selected with a presumption that as so-called large firms they were making the mainstream and had some influence on others among the industry or Japanese firms at large, symbolically at least, in terms of adoptions and usages of their HR practices. A questionnaire was attached to the letters, which asked about types of employment, the number of employees in each category, types of employees who have the possibility of personnel transfer and *tenkin* in their career, reasons for *tenkin*, purposes of *tenkin*, *tenkin*-related allowances, *tenkin*-related systems for actors and for spouses, and stipulations of *tenkin* as regulation. I received a reply from only one firm. A HR staff seemed to have filled in the questionnaire, but denied me an interview because they had just begun a new HR system and not yet assessed its effect. I do not refer to this questionnaire in this book, because only a few data selected or written on that meant little from a qualitative study's point of view. The rest of the fifteen firms remained silent.

Seeking firms who could cooperate with my research, I visited several informants to ask for introductions. Eventually, two different informants introduced me to two firms. One of these contacts was extended to another firm by snowball sampling. I also obtained appointments with two firms by direct inquiries. Interviews with these five firms were conducted between July 2015 and March 2016. Later in February 2017, I had the chance to visit one of the five firms for a follow-up interview, as well as additional two firms, in the course of fieldwork for a DAAD (Deutscher Akademischer Austauschdienst) joint study on "Labor market diversification and its risk in Japan."

All the interviews were conducted at the firms' head offices with HR managers, for one hour at minimum or over two hours at the longest, using the questionnaire and a list of questions. I sent the questionnaire by email in advance to these firms, so that all the managers could prepare for the interviews. In the second round that I conducted in 2017, I did not use the questionnaire but only asked about their practice verbally. In both rounds, I also asked questions about other issues such as women and foreign workers' employment. All the interviews were recorded and later transcribed, and then analyzed by myself by attempting to find out the similarities and differences of the firms' practices of *tenkin*.

The seven firms consisted of five manufacturers located in Tokyo, Kyoto, Osaka, and Hiroshima Prefectures, and one insurance company and one newspaper company both based in central Tokyo. All the companies had operated their businesses over fifty years, and most of them had histories of more than a century. They had branches and related companies both nationwide and worldwide. Pseudonyms are used in this book.

The Individuals

The second approach consisted of qualitative interviews with individuals who worked as dual-career [*tomobataraki*] couples and had the experience of *tenkin* of their own and/or spouses. Using a flier and a snowball sampling method, I obtained access to fifty-four people who were married and had experienced *tenkin* as workers and/or as spouses. In order to concentrate my focus on the new actors of *tenkin*, I narrowed the group to forty-six married workers, forty women and six men, who were aged between twenty-seven and fifty, and worked full-time for companies located in Japan. Most of the men were introduced by the wives. Among the forty-six workers, four women and four men had experiences of their own *tenkin* only, while thirteen women and one man had experiences of their own and spouses' *tenkin*. The rest of twenty-three women and one man had experiences of their spouses' *tenkin* only.

It took more than two years from December 2014 through to March 2017 to meet all of the interviewees. This was due to two factors. First and foremost, such dual-career couples, who had experienced *tenkin* of their own and/or spouses and who had continued working full-time seemed to be very rare in Japan. To find the interviewees, I used my lifelong network that included old friends and distant acquaintances who lived in various cities both nationwide and worldwide. When I asked them about the possibility of introductions, I was usually told that they had never heard of such cases of dual-career couples who had experience of *tenkin*. The second reason was technical. I had to wait for one informant until the time she returned to Japan from her husband's overseas *tenkin*, because I conducted all the interviews face to face. Almost all of the interviews were held over one year between January 2015 and February 2016.

The interviews were conducted basically one by one, except for a few joint interviews of a husband and wife, and co-workers. The venues were cafés or restaurants where I met the interviewees during their lunch times, or their houses or workplaces, according to their requests. The duration was one hour on average, ranging from forty minutes to two hours. I used two kinds of questionnaires, one for those who experienced their own *tenkin* and another for those who only experienced their spouses' *tenkin*, aiming to obtain basic information about their work and family including some information about *tenkin*. It included their age, education, work, job category, year and type of entry, detailed information of their current job such as a position, job, role, the number of co-workers, working hours, income[6], past trajectories of *tenkin* including where, when, and for what job they and/or their spouses were transferred, their spouses' job, the number and ages of children, and about their home ownership. When we met, I soon asked the interviewees to fill in the questionnaire. Based on a list of questions I had prepared, I asked them why and how they made decisions in each event of their public and domestic experiences. In addition, at the end of the interviews, I posed one simple question to all: "What does *tenkin* mean to you?" This aimed at interpreting their narratives from the anthropological point of view, as Gordon Mathews (2003) did in his research about meanings of men's lives. The interviews were recorded, except for two cases in which the interviews suddenly started before I had the chance to ask if I could record. The recordings were later transcribed and analyzed by myself. I attempted to find patterns of the informants' consciousness and actions from the data.

Among the forty-six interviewees, thirty-one (67 percent) were in their thirties. Some had bachelor's degrees, others had master's degrees from top-tier universities, and two were graduates of two-year colleges. Ten women had changed their jobs, once at most, to seek better careers. At the time of the interviews, they lived at various cities in the greater Tokyo and Osaka areas, and Aichi and Hiroshima Prefectures, with experiences of having lived in various cities including overseas due to *tenkin*. All of the couples took the men's surname, while many of the women informally kept their natal surname in their work and even during our interviews as well. Two of the forty couples lived with the women's natal parents. Thirty-one of them had children, four at most. Yet, only three women had experienced their own *tenkin* as mothers, and one, Ms. Kawano, had eventually changed her job due to a work-life conflict caused by *tenkin*. Another woman, Ms. Nishino, aged fifty, had her *tenkin* after her daughter became eighteen years old and started to live alone in order to go to university located distant from home. She said that she had asked her firm to delay sending her for *tenkin*, or what she called *tanshin funin*, until the time. The other woman, Ms. Hino, aged thirty-nine, was my key informant, who navigated her life as a career-track worker and mother as she desired through the practice of *tenkin*. Pseudonyms are used throughout this book.

Social Events

The last approach was participant observation in events related to this research. It included recruiting events for job-hunting students held in Waseda University and public study events initiated by Nikkei Newspaper Company and non-profit organizations. The purposes for this fieldwork were to understand the meaning of the practice of *tenkin* in the society at large and to learn ordinary people's attitudes toward the dynamics of the transition arising contemporary Japan. I took fieldnotes in all the sites and analyzed them.

From participation in the "*Ikubosu* [caring bosses] Seminar" held by an NPO called Fathering Japan[7], I acquired great insights that satisfy my purposes for this approach. The NPO Fathering Japan was established in 2006 by several male workers. Most of the original members were in leading and managerial positions of large companies. In the beginning, their focuses were placed on promoting *ikumen* [caring fathers] campaigns with a slogan, "Let's become smiling fathers!" (NPO Fathering Japan 2023). The organization started the "*Ikubosu* Project" in 2014, when they became aware of the necessities of having and developing such bosses to push the *ikumen* project forward. *Ikubosu* refers to "managers who consider work-life balance of their co-workers, support the workers' careers and lives, achieve the business results in their workplaces, and also enjoy their own work and private life" (NPO Fathering Japan 2023). Since 2014, the organization have held *ikubosu* seminars numerous times nationwide. I participated in the seminars twice, in February 2016 in Hiroshima Prefecture, and February 2017 in Hyogo Prefecture. Both seminars were hosted and organized by the local city governments. As in a flier, the meeting aimed to train *ikubosu*. Anyone who was interested in the theme was welcome. Both seminars consisted of lectures by members of the NPO and workshops by participants to create their own action plan to become *ikubosu*. The 2017 seminar was divided into two days. This was initiated by the manager at the Gender Equality Bureau of the city, who wished for the participants to put their action plans into practice in their real workplaces after the first seminar, and then share the outcomes in the second meeting. In the end of the complete program, participants were given a certificate. There were thirty participants and most of them, except for seven public workers of the city, were managers or workers of HR departments at various companies in the local city. For the participation, I identified myself as a doctoral researcher studying *tenkin*.

CHAPTER OUTLINE

The body of this book is divided into six parts. Chapters 1 and 2 elaborate on how Japanese firms conduct *tenkin*. Chapters 3–5 explain how workers, including potential workers in chapter 3, think about and go through *tenkin* in their lives. In the latter chapters focusing on the individuals, I describe the "serious games" (Ortner 2006: 144) of the informants one by one, to elucidate "the intense play of multiply positioned subjects pursuing cultural goals within a matrix of local inequalities and power differentials" (Ortner 2006: 144). By doing so, I attempt to provide a full picture of my informants' career management.

HR managers' descriptions about *tenkin* in chapters 1 and 2 reveal how contemporary Japanese firms are efficiency seekers and gender oriented. *Tenkin* was taken for granted by the HR managers I interviewed, who had different backgrounds in different firms. They utilize *tenkin*'s purposeful features in their employment systems. These are skill development, training, and custom, all of which are responsible for the existence and determination of the administrative rules of the ILM. With these systems in mind, the HR managers tended to express gendered assumptions, for example, on family formation due to *tenkin*. Chapter 2 elucidates the practices which the firms I interviewed had taken over the several years before I started my research. Some of them developed and changed the practice of *tenkin* and its related practices. Two manufacturers incorporated a social movement of "diversity and inclusion" and attempted to implement *tenkin* for more women. They create new systems for their employees to balance *tenkin* and family lives. The result is that these attempts are likely to help to boost careers of their female workers little by little.

Chapter 3 begins spotlighting individual people' experiences in *tenkin*. As a starter, I describe how job-hunting students viewed the practice of *tenkin*. They saw *tenkin*, if it is overseas, as a great chance for their career development. This positive prospect was more or less applied to most of my informants, while they were young career seekers, mostly in their 20s. During the early stages of their careers, even after the couples married, some men and women enjoyed going along with *tenkin*, mostly of their husbands. They had little negotiation and tension with others in their workplaces and homes in their decision-making processes. But, once women gave birth to a child, their family responsibilities became incompatible with their own and husbands' *tenkin*. For dual-career couples, balancing their jobs that involve *tenkin* and domestic care responsibilities is still not easy in contemporary Japan.

Chapter 4 sheds light on the career management of dual-career couples who decided to live separately due to *tenkin*. This pattern included the cases of their own *tenkin* and husbands' *tenkin*, mostly in their 30s or over. During their separation, the couples commonly desired and fostered independent marital relationships. Separation is a trigger for individuals to exert agency in pursuit and enactment of a better life in *tenkin*. But for couples who were at the final stage of their reproductive ages, the separation became less and less attractive or productive for them. If the couples had a child, it often made the working mothers susceptible to taking "exit options" (Schoppa 2006) from jobs with *tenkin*. These couples' lives clearly suggest that working mothers are more vulnerable to the ILM's logic in contemporary Japan.

Chapter 5 explores the lives of dual-career couples who decided to collaborate in their own or husbands' *tenkin*. The practice of moving together in spouses' *tenkin* used to be described as "following." But the women I featured in this chapter did not show the disposition of dependency, on their spouse in the cultural meaning. They strived to take advantage of the practices of *tenkin* to live better lives. This intention was stronger when *tenkin* was to overseas. During the co-living period, moreover, the couples held more interactions within the marriage as well as with others in their workplaces and developed less-gendered relationships with the people surrounding them. With these various new resources and collaborative relationships, the couples managed their careers, while facing various new roadblocks.

I conclude with a discussion on the structure of *tenkin* and its possibility of change, the dual-career couples' work and family lives, the necessity for the labor market reform, and the meanings of "Career Management."

NOTES

1. This is *tenkin* in which the worker's family does not follow him/her. I use this term *tanshin funin*, instead of English, for two reasons: first, because the term cannot be rendered by an accurate simple English word; and further because the term embodies a cultural meaning that a transferee has to accept *tenkin* even if his family should live separately, as I shall describe in this book.

2. A process industry [*sōchi sangyō*] represents steel industry and chemical industry that process law materials through a series of a chemical process (Yamamoto 1967).

3. The work rules book plays a substantial role in actual workplaces. I argue this in chapter 1, using my empirical data.

4. There are some terms to describe a wife in the Japanese language, which are used in different occasions and contexts. *Nyōbō* literally means a "woman in a room," which includes other meanings such as a court lady. *Kanai* and *okusan* have similar connotations as *nyōbō* in terms that it literally means "inside a house" and "someone inside" or "someone domestic" from the feminist point of view. *Yome* is a bride in a *ie* family, but can refer to a wife with few senses of the *ie* system. *Tsuma* should be a straight translation of an English "wife." There are corresponding terms in describing a husband in the Japanese language: *teishu*, *shujin*, *danna*, *muko*, and *otto*.

5. A Japanese singer Seiko Matsuda sang "Red Sweet Pea" in NHK (Japan Broadcasting Corporation)'s New Year's Eve Annual Singers' Contest in 2015, whose

melody is famous for "I will follow you." *Anata ni tsuite ikitai* [I want to follow you] has been a powerful love message ever since the song was firstly released in 1982.

6. I only asked income of those who had experienced their own *tenkin*, with assumption that the income level differed according to their experiences of *tenkin*, for instance, the places, positions, durations, and so on, and therefore, the answers would help me understand more about the practice of *tenkin*. Sixteen of twenty-two interviewees (seventeen women and five men) who had their own *tenkin* responded and the income level ranged from four million yen to more than ten million yen a year. Contrary to the assumption, I saw few correlations in their income and *tenkin*, except for the possible relevance of their income and seniority, so that I do not discuss them in this book. Yet, since very few studies have covered Japanese workers' income and its overall relations with and influences on their lives, further investigations are called for. For the income gaps between those who have *tenkin* and others, see Sato, Hashimoto, and Owan (2019).

7. The name of the NPO is only real in this book. I have got permission from Mr. Seto, one of the founders of the NPO and my informant. He told me to publish his real name, too, but I used a pseudonym here for him, in the same ways as other interviewees.

Chapter 1

The Practice Taken for Granted

My qualitative research revealed that *tenkin* is a critical, purposeful practice for large firms in contemporary Japan. HR managers' implementation of *tenkin* and explanations about its mechanisms evidenced the existence of the Internal Labor Market (ILM) in contemporary Japanese society. As previously mentioned, three major factors of the ILM: skill specificity, on-the-job training, and customary law (Doeringer and Piore 1971: 13–27) are embodied in *tenkin*. In the market, where the establishment and development went hand in hand with the gendered division of labor in Japan, *tenkin* also enabled the smooth running of personnel systems for male breadwinners in Japan.

THE INTERNAL LABOR MARKET IN CONTEMPORARY JAPAN

The employers at the four companies I studied strongly emphasized human resource development or career development of their employees, as the major purpose of *tenkin*. The practice of HR development, which was also marked as the top answer in the above-noted JILPT (2017) research, in fact, included a lot of specific practices. The main two of them are training and fostering skills, which are defined by on-the-job training and skill specificity in the theory of the ILM. Moreover, as employees come to acquire specific skills, they become the subjects of *tenkin* for another purpose, which is appropriate deployment. Two companies provided this answer. For the practice to take place, there seemed to be a certain agreement necessary in the organization to judge "who is appropriate." It was the custom that each organization had fostered. This section elucidates how the employers take in these practices through *tenkin*, in contemporary white-collar workplaces.

On-the-Job Training

Tenkin provides on-the-job training for white-collar workers. This type of training is usually provided for newly hired workers in the initial stage of building their careers. For example, in Tachibana Newspaper Company Ltd., hereafter *Tachibana* Newspaper, the training period was called "*shugyō kikan*." Through the transfers implemented one after another in a few-year interval, trainees learn specific skills that are necessary for their daily, as well as future jobs in publishing newspapers. These skills cannot be acquired by formal costly training programs. It has to be conducted in *genba* [field].

Tachibana Newspaper Company Ltd. was one of the biggest nationwide newspaper companies in Japan. I visited Tachibana's head office building in Tokyo in December 2015. A HR manager, Mr. Kimura, an administrative and HR vice-director, Mr. Tanaka, and an editorial writer, Mr. Hosoda were my interviewees. As I encountered in most of the companies, the receptionists were women. The newspaper company hired approximately 2,400 regular employees. This employment category included several jobs such as writers, sales persons, and technicians, whoever were hired as full-time, long-term-employed workers. Mr. Kimura mentioned that all of them had possibilities of transfers over their entire working life. The "transfers" he mentioned meant *idō* that the firm generally used in their HR management based on their work rules [*shūgyō kisoku*]. The term, *tenkin* is used only for operational reasons, when, for example, a transferee was required to move his/her house due to transfer [*idō*] and thereby was eligible for *tenkin*-related allowances. Otherwise, they use the term, transfer [*idō*] to describe *tenkin*, too.

Writers had transfers that resulted in *tenkin* most frequently among the jobs in the regular employment scheme. Those who were in sales and technical jobs also had *tenkin* but merely between head offices[1] and less frequently. Mr. Kimura said that writers, particularly when they were young, needed to be trained through frequent transfers between local branches. The period was more or less five years. During that time, young writers experience several different departments that deal with police offices, city offices, prefectural offices, and sports. They learn how to collect data and report on different types of people, instructed by their seniors. This developed their skills to handle all major areas of news as an "independent writer" [*ichininmae no kisha*], according to Mr. Hosoda, an editorial writer. Only after the training period, could these writers "come back" to the head office by *tenkin* to narrow their specialty and handle bigger news which would be published nationwide. This practice of training and ensuing transfers and *tenkin* were all taken for granted by the managers.

In all the manufacturers, career-track jobs posed the requirement of *tenkin*. One of the practices of *tenkin* was to deploy workers for their early-career training. It is called initial deployment [*shoki haizoku*] in these firms. The workers are sent to domestic, often local offices and plants, which are usually called *genba* [field]. They are expected to acquire the basic knowledge of production.

For example, Motomachi Manufacturing Co. Ltd, hereafter Motomachi Manufacturing, the Kansai-based company producing and selling electronic devices, sent almost all of their newly recruited career-track workers to local factories for short-term training. The manufacturer had 30,000 employees on a consolidated basis. Around 7,000 were regular employees and among them, 3,000 career-track employees had possibilities of *tenkin* to any sites of the company during their working life. In terms of the initial training, the duration differed from a few weeks to several months depending on what year the workers joined the firm. It seemed that the situation of the global economy and business affected how Motomachi put transfers into practice. I will raise this point in the next section.

Hiroo Manufacturing Company Ltd., hereafter Hiroo Manufacturing, also conducted the *tenkin* of newly employed workers for training. The company made machines for food production. It had a history of more than hundred years. The head office and main factories were in Hiroshima Prefecture, while sales offices were located nationwide and worldwide. The company had almost 3,000 employees on a consolidated basis. Among them, about 1,000 employees were hired for the headquarters and nearly 750 "global employees [formerly career-track employees]," sales persons in particular, had possibilities of *tenkin*. When new employees enter the company in April, they have one-month formal training period in the head office. Then in May, by *tenkin*, most of the male employees scatter [*chirabaru*] at once. The female employees stay another one year (at the head office). "During that time, they are expected to study hard," Ms. Watabe, a female manager said. The women tended to be sent to sales office, but only a few handled sales jobs in the same way as men. Ms. Watabe added, "Perhaps, the female employees are treated with kid gloves [*daiji ni suru*] by our company. If they were assigned to the sales job, their boss would have difficulty in treating them (in the job generally handled by men)." The firm differentiated the way of training by gender.

Obviously, Hiroo Manufacturing put "protection of women [*josei hogo*]" into practice, although Ms. Watabe did not use the term, but only implied it. The protection of women, or *bosei hogo*, was to protect women in workplaces with a view that women bear children and therefore need protection. That protection was originally stipulated in 1947 Labor Standard Law. In 1999, however, it was revised, associated with the revision of the EEOL (Equal Employment Opportunity Law). Female workers became allowed to work overtime and the nightshift. But, even though almost two decades have passed since then, people's behavior has little changed in the manufacturer.

34   Chapter 1

If the early-career on-the-job training is provided for women later than men, the HR development of the female workers is delayed.

Okamoto Insurance Company Ltd., hereafter Okamoto Insurance, also transferred their career-track workers for the purpose of on-the-job training, although a manager I interviewed, Mr. Satō, did not clearly state the terms. Okamoto Insurance was one of the major general insurance companies in Japan. Among the 20,000 employees of Okamoto Insurance, approximately 5,000 all-area employees, mostly men, had frequent *tenkin*. The firm placed importance on "relocating a right person to a right place [*tekizai tekisho no haichi*]." It was to rotate the (career-track) all-area employees among positions located nationwide as fairly as possible. This practice was indispensable for the firm as it helped the employees learn differences among branches, through which they could accumulate experiences. Mr. Satō even added:

> From my own experience, *tenkin* makes us feel easy [*raku*], because relocation to a different environment, even if it is a company's order, makes us try hard, change ourselves, and improve our ability. In your first and second years in the new assignment, you may feel everything new and stimulating, but soon after that, you must feel this way (gesturing declining with his hand). Transfers can get over it (the decline of ability). If we can do so without *tenkin*, it might be a good idea. But we cannot expect that in our company (which has branches and offices everywhere).

Through the practice of *tenkin*, Okamoto Insurance materialized various purposes such as not only on-the-job training but also ability and skill development, and appropriate deployment, making more sense of the long-term employment, mostly for male employees.

Skill Development

Almost all of the HR managers noted that *tenkin* enables workers to acquire skills. As in Doeringer and Piore's (1971) theory of the ILM, the skills were not only required in their daily jobs and but also valued for upward mobility, while helping to cut the cost and improve efficiency in the firm. In the ILM theory, this was called skill specificity and entitled as one factor of the market. The initial training above helped both employers and employees find what skills the employees have to specialize in and develop. Then the workers stepped into their mid-career stage. Behind the theory, there was always a premise of long-term employment.

Kamisato Manufacturing Company Ltd., hereafter Kamisato Manufacturing, for example, conducted *tenkin* for skill development as its most crucial purpose, and differentiated the frequencies and spans of *tenkin*, depending on the employees' specialization. Kamisato produced components for industrial machinery and automobiles, and its sales records were top in the market. The manufacturer has a history of over a hundred years. Since the early stage of its postwar recovery, it had expanded its business overseas. At the time of the interview, it situated plants and offices in over thirty countries on all continents. Two employees from its department of HR development were my interviewees, Ms. Meguro, the HR manager and a Ph.D. student at one of the universities in Tokyo, and Mr. Kudō, the section chief.

The career-track employees could be divided into two different categories: technical staff [*gijutsu kei*] and office-based staff [*jimu kei*], a distinction which other manufacturers also adopted. The difference was attributed to specializations of the workers at college and university. The technical staff was also divided into two types: engineers and technicians. The former dealt with production development, as Ms. Meguro described them as "technique of the technique [*gijutsu no gijutsu*]." Basically they were deployed in two major plants and had *tenkin* only between these sites, if any. The latter, technicians, or *gijutsuya* in Ms. Meguro's term, handled production engineering in the plants located all over the world. So, they were most likely to have *tenkin* among its employees. Ms. Meguro said that over 80 percent of the career-track employees, whose proportion was common to other firms in the same industry, could consist of technicians in the company, although they were also intended to experience office-related jobs. Finally, the office-based staff included administrative jobs and sales jobs. Some of them, even though they had majored in humanities or social sciences, could be assigned production engineering jobs that required *tenkin* after they entered the company.

Trajectories of *tenkin*, which career-track technicians generally had, were different, depending on what products they handled. One employee had been sent to plants in the United Kingdom and then to South Korea in the early stage of his career. Another worker had *tenkin* to Brazil for over ten years for production management there. Mr. Kudō said that, although the actual duration of *tenkin* varied from person to person, also depending on which products and jobs he/she dealt with, it was generally five years for those who were accompanied by their family. For those who moved alone [*tanshin funin*], the duration of *tenkin* was supposed to be three years, as the employers had to "consider [*hairyo*]" the transferees' family issues due to the separation, Ms. Meguro added. The shorter period for *tanshin funin* was regulated by a request from the company union. Yet all in all, the company's practice clarified the corporate-oriented feature of the practices of *tenkin*.

Motomachi Manufacturing, the company of producing and selling electronic devices, also noted that *tenkin* was for "HR development." I visited the company twice in July 2015 and February 2017. In my initial interview, two male managers, a vice president, Mr. Tsuchida, and senior manager, Mr. Koyanagi, of the HR department, invited me to a cozy drawing room with a set of black leather sofas. The vice president, Mr. Tsuchida, was present in the 2017 follow-up interview with another HR manager, Mr. Ueda. In Motomachi, among 50,000 workers employed on a consolidated basis, 4,000 career-track workers had possibilities of *tenkin*. It was to "enhance a worker's abilities, skills, and volitions, leading the firm to make more profits," the vice president, Mr. Tsuchida said. Recently, China was more and more common for overseas *tenkin*, since the firm had offices and factories there to make the local personnel produce the products.

Given this business situation, the practice of *tenkin* was unique. Both Mr. Tsuchida and Mr. Koyanagi emphasized their practice of intimate communication in the workplace. Before unofficial announcement [*naiji*][2], there was supposed to be some informal communication between the manager and transferee. For example, they had systems of personnel evaluation, ability evaluation, or sales evaluation, roughly three opportunities that the employee could talk with his boss under the name of feedback. On such occasions, the manager was supposed to ask the recent situation of the employee. Other than these systems, they should also have daily chances of communicating with each other. The recent situation included private conditions such as building a house, implying that the employee did not want to move anywhere else for now. The managers insisted that the employees feel free to tell any issues to their boss and the boss may respond to employees, "OK then, let's blow it (any offer) off (if it comes)!" Mr. Tsuchida added the following explanation to the situation:

> We do so because we think that if the employee is not willing to transfer, he cannot provide his best performance. So sometimes, there is an employee who is not willing to accept transfer, while his managers want him in that position for business needs. In such a case, his boss will make every effort to change his mind. We regard such cases as beneficial to him as well to bring out his ability. Actually, we rarely have complaints regarding transfers. Transfer is our culture, and we take it for granted like the climate [*fūdo*][3]. So I don't think everyone has a feeling of resistance. Sometimes we hear a request from the worker's side, "I have been in this position for five years so I want to move."

Although Motomachi shared reasons and purposes for *tenkin* with other companies, their practice of *tenkin*, particularly the way of appointment and its premise, was distinct. In Motomachi, apparently, negotiation over careers including *tenkin* between employers and workers was a daily, welcome practice, and this was their norm.

How can we interpret the "intimate communication" in Motomachi, which the manager insisted on? It sounded like "negotiation" between employers and workers, although the managers did not use the term. Generally, workplace negotiation is supposed to be held between employers and representatives of workers, ideally unions. However, in its practice of *tenkin*, the workers in Motomachi were required to negotiate alone, daily, or in appraisal. Through the practice, workers needed to speak up about their wishes not only in their careers but in their families as well and show their commitment to the work and company more than the family. Then by the appraisal, whether satisfactory or disappointing, the workers were informed of the results of their negotiation, so that they would build strategies for their next negotiations. With these functions of negotiation, *tenkin* in Motomachi was put into practice, as if it had been something volunteered by workers. It is likely that this strong *tenkin* culture inhibited women from climbing in the ranks: the rate of women in its managerial positions was 2 percent (Toyo Keizai Shinposha 2014). The company was thoroughly male dominated.

In our follow-up interview, Mr. Tsuchida claimed that the firm had seldom ever had a strategy in doing their business. They "merely make electronic parts that can be used for next-generation products," and this was how the firm "has caught up with the global business environment and increased the profits for the past decades." To be prepared for those coming products itself might be their strategy to survive, though. To this end, the firm needed skilled workers who could anticipate their business and develop and sell their products both nationwide and worldwide for a certain long term. Also, this purpose resulted in the workers' career development through *tenkin*. To figure out who could be responsible and ready for this, frequent intimate communication was essential for each party. When anyone was acknowledged as skilled, negotiation was conducted on the assumption that he would subjectively assert his desire for *tenkin* with a sense of responsibility developed in Motomachi's climate [*fūdo*]. Here, corporate interests in the global business competition mattered. For employers in this environment, training and skill development through *tenkin* seemed to be regarded as natural things in life.

Custom

That way of thinking was solidified by customs all companies shared. Custom, or a customary law as "an unwritten set of rules based largely upon past practice or precedent" (Doeringer and Piore 1971: 23), was present as a screen in the interpretation and implementation of the work rules [*shūgyō kisoku*]. When training and skill development were carried out inside a work group, employment become more stable and the same workers came into regular and repeated contact with each other, generating and experiencing unwritten rules. The process increasingly made the market internalized and less responsive to dynamic economic forces in the external labor market, as Doeringer and Piore (1971: 13–40) noted.

Chapter 1

The financial industries had a tendency to implement *tenkin* periodically and mandatorily for a certain reason, which was not written anywhere. Okamoto Insurance, for example, also addressed one top purpose for *tenkin* as "career development." By sending the right person to the right place, the company attempted to develop employees' careers and this way was believed as efficient for both the firm as well as for the employees. In order for the rotation to go smoothly, Mr. Satō mentioned that a training and career program for the employee in each position was made to finish within around five years, so that other staff in the office could send the employee to his next position and welcome a new employee routinely. This meant that Okamoto's management of employees' career development was regulated rigidly, while also being unlimited, in terms of where and how many times they were to be transferred.

There was another reason for this regulated, unlimited *tenkin*. It was for a belief, or discourse, that frequent *tenkin* could "avoid corruption [*fusei no bōshi*]" caused by "adhesion [*yuchaku*]," possibly attributed to business relationships that were too close and too long. Mr. Satō mentioned this point that "as we are a financial institution, placing an employee in one particular position for many years does not sound good (to others)." This statement implied that other financial institutions also took this practice of *tenkin* as common sense, as I often heard during my fieldwork, too. For these financial firms, *tenkin* was indispensable to maintain their own logic of crime prevention under long-term employment. More specifically, flexible *tenkin* helped to keep personnel efficiency of the industry as a whole.

In practice, Okamoto ordered *tenkin* every Spring. Beforehand, the HR department checked the self-declaration sheets every fall through to winter. Generally, in October, employees and their bosses had consultations to share their wishes for transfers. On February 28 or March 1, the company had a day for unofficial announcement [*naiji*] to inform the employees about their transfers, usually, the new positions and reasons for them. Then a "large movement of people [*minzoku daiidō*]"[4] would take place on April 1, Mr. Satō noted.

But, the reasons that the employees were told were not always authentic. To my question about whether the company had a practice of feedback in their declaration system, Mr. Satō implied one purpose of *tenkin*, "stringing along," which I noted in Introduction:

> There is no stipulation anywhere requiring bosses to give explanations about the transfers. Practically, though, I think they do, just as I myself used to do when I was a manager. First, I asked the HR department why (my juniors were assigned to certain positions). Then, I tried to tell my juniors anything that could cheer them up, like, "This job has been looking for someone like you. You are

selected for it!" [*kimi ni shiraha no ya ga tattannda*]. In our company, the HR department may have more power (than the field managers).

There are very few cases of refusals by employees. Very few, or none. If we have such cases often, we would be troubled, because we are transferring employees like a puzzle. This person should go there, that person should come here, and so on. If the second person stops at his position, we need to find another person to fill in the position here, right? And the next question is, what are we going to do with that second person, isn't it? So, we rarely have rejections. This is because, as I showed you in the work rules book, *the workers have to accept transfers and they cannot reject the transfers without good reasons*. For the good reasons, some workers have tried to threaten to resign: "Otherwise, I will quit." Such cases, although rare, have been understood not as rejection, but as quitting. We have them, for instance, once in a few years at most.

Mr. Satō's claim about a puzzle was the idea that had been adopted as a judicial precedent since the 1986 TOA Paint Case. In the case, the Supreme Court acknowledged the validity of the company's control over playing the puzzle and determined employees' disadvantages in family lives as normal inconveniences. Okamoto Insurance used this logic and exercised its ruling power with the work rules book and the custom to interpret it.

Work rules are a set of regulations that employers, with ten employees or more, must prescribe for their employees in every office unit, according to Article 89 of the Japanese Labor Standards Law. Since the rules are written in a book, or booklet, the work rules usually refer to the book. The Japanese Ministry of Health, Labor, and Welfare (MHLW 2023) specifies the significance of the work rules book as follows:

It is important for every workplace, regardless of its size or industry, to establish a bright and safe environment for workers. To this end, by clarifying working hours and wages, as well as working conditions and labor standards such as personnel and office regulations on a work rules book, employers must try to avoid troubles that their employees may have. (MHLW 2023: 2)

This stipulation implies that the book itself is NOT a contract, but only a one-way promise by employers to employees. Actually, employers are merely required to disseminate the book by making posters or putting work rules online, so that employees can make access anytime they want to, and once employers disseminate the book to employees in any form, the rules become valid (MHLW 2023: 4). This procedure suggests that, although the significance above appears that the book aims to protect employees in their workplaces, it rather seems to function to give legitimacy to employers to implement any written practices.

That said, in order to avoid the oppressive use of the rules, the Japanese Labor Standards Law sets three conditions on employers' implementation of work rules books (MHLW 2018: 2–4). First, by the Article 89, the government regulates some of the clauses to be written in work rules books. They firstly include "indispensable clauses [*zettai hitsuyō kisai jikō*]," which prescribe working hours and holidays, wages, and retirement. The other items are called "relatively necessary clauses [*sōtaiteki hitsuyō kisai jikō*]." In these clauses, employers must stipulate regulations about allowance of retirement, temporary and minimum wages, cost burden on workers, health-and-safety-related issues, training, disaster or sick compensation, commendation and punishment, and other rules applied to all employees. In the last clause of "other rules," regulations about personnel transfers and *tenkin* are generally stipulated. In addition to these clauses prescribed by Article 89, there are also things that employers can specify voluntarily, including special statements or philosophy.

The MHLW (2023) model work rules book presents the sample clause regarding transfer as follows:

> Clause 8 A company may order [*meizuru kotoga aru*] employees to change the place of work or the job they do when it is necessary for business [*gyōmujō hitsuyō ga aru baaini*].
> 2. The company may transfer [*shukkō saseru kotoga aru*] employees to its related companies while retaining them as employees when it is necessary for business.
> 3. In the case of 2, employees cannot reject the order without good reason [*seitō na riyū naku kore wo kobamukoto wa dekinai*]. (MHLW 2023: 14)

On the model clause, the government backs up employers' rights to transfer employees as they wish, although the auxiliary verb of "may" sounds uncertain. This policy is obvious in its additional note in the model work rules book as follows:

> In order to avoid troubles occurring by unsatisfactory transfers, a company is encouraged to stipulate this clause (Clause 8) in its work rules book. Of course, it goes without saying that it is important for the company to obtain consent [*dōi*] from employees (when it implements transfers). (MHLW 2023: 15)

This weak stipulation and the vague meaning of "consent" suggest that "unsatisfactory transfers" can happen.

The second condition of the work rules, which is also specified by Article 89, is employers' requirement to submit their books to jurisdictional Labor Standards Bureaus. Also, when employers attempt to change regulations, by Article 90 of the law, they are requested to obtain approval from representatives of their employees' absolute majority, usually union members if any, and then re-submit the revised document to the jurisdictional Labor Standards Bureaus.

The third condition is to limit the extent of enforcement of work rules by Article 92 of the law. It clarifies that any work rule book must not contravene other labor laws and union agreement [*rōdō kyōyaku*]. A union agreement is a contract made through collective bargaining between employers and union members, and it always takes precedence over the work rules. In other words, from the judicial point of view, unions are able to bargain the labor conditions specified in the work rules books.

In fact, two manufacturers, Kamisato and Motomachi, clearly stated that their corporate unions actively committed to the restructure of the practice of *tenkin*. For example, Kamisato attempted a radical change of the system that stipulates the workers' requirement of *tenkin*. But it ended up in vain. Motomachi's unions pushed the company to adopt a *tenkin*-related system, which allowed workers to follow their spouse's *tenkin* overseas. But it did not lead to fundamental change. I will describe Motomachi's case in Chapter 2.

The corporate union of Kamisato Manufacturing, the Kanto-based maker of components for industrial machinery and automobiles, seemed to be relatively active. It functioned for obtaining better working conditions, if not entirely. As I discussed in Introduction, unions in Japanese workplaces are different from those in Western countries in general. The primary feature is their cooperative attitudes to management. Historically, as Gordon (1985) elucidated, blue-collar workers in manufacturers exerted labor power to their employers, complaining that their working conditions were "3K" (*Kitsui Kitanai Kiken*), or demanding, dirty, and dangerous, jobs, as Mr. Kudō also mentioned. Huge battles took place right after World War II, in Toshiba and Nissan Corporations, for example. During that time, however, the management side finally began listening to the union's voices, rather than thrusting them aside, to take more advantage of personnel costs. Ever since the 1950s, when these workers began to obtain membership in their companies, they became willing to cooperate with the management, hoping to make their quality of life better. In this dynamic, the practice of *tenkin* won its legitimacy, seen as an indispensable practice for both firms and employees, and became a habitude of Japanese business practice. However in Kamisato, a manufacturer lasting over a hundred years, labor-management negotiation seemed still to be carried out.

Their bargaining process was as follows, according to Mr. Kudō. Every year, before the labor-management negotiation, the union sent questionnaires to all union members to collect their voices. In the meantime, the members could also ask for a one-on-one interview with their managers. This action is also allowed when the union members found some problems with regard to *tenkin*. Through these actions, convenience for the management and rights for the workers, which were often at odds, were negotiated for the best outcome. The actual bargaining also seemed to be helped by an industry union, which is part of Rengō (Japanese Trade Union Confederation), where Kamisato Manufacturing's union members could share their labor situations as well as issues horizontally, and find solutions by listening to other cases. Kamisato's union seemed to function as the collective body to challenge their employers.

With regard to the *tenkin* system, Mr. Kudō told me an episode of its union's attempt to abolish *tenkin*, or at least to make the employers limit places where the workers were sent. To this end, the union negotiated to reorganize the categories of career-track employment to corporate staff and field staff. The latter scheme was similar to that of an area-based or regional employee category without nationwide *tenkin*, which other firms in this study had also installed recently for their organizational reforms. For the management side, *tenkin* was necessary, not only for the development the workers' managerial skills but also for future possible business restructuring. As the company has expanded its business overseas over decades, they cannot promise that all of its domestic business will continue. "Though this is my imagination," Mr. Kudō said, "the management side should have anticipated inconvenience possibly happening in the case of such business restructuring if they set and limit places where their employees work." The last resort in the collective negotiation (between the employers and union members), therefore, became the installation of the new category, the field staff, who would specialize in certain products. By separating the products to handle in this way, the workers could limit their areas to work, to the extent possible. This did not mean they would not have *tenkin* anymore. They would, but only between limited regional offices.

But the reorganization had not gone well, Mr. Kudō added. Because the company continued to treat corporate staff, the former career-track employees, as those who were supposed to experience as many jobs and offices as possible to develop their managerial skills, the field staff were seen as halfway career seekers. In other words, the management of Kamisato needed career-track employees who could be able to move and work whenever the company required. The field staff barely met this need. Mr. Kudō remarked, therefore, the category of the field staff had not taken root as expected, and the company had hired few new graduates into this category. Despite the union's efforts, the career-track category had been re-unified and remained one, which required nationwide and worldwide *tenkin* to seek promotion to managers. The case of Kamisato Manufacturing indicates how *tenkin* satisfies its firm's various purposes in contemporary white-collar workers' workplaces with the backup of the work rules and norms. It enables skill development as well as employment security for workers on one hand, and efficient management for employers on the other hand.

Similarly, Hiroo Manufacturing had adopted a new employment category through its personnel reform conducted in 2002, attempting to distinguish their workers who would accept nationwide *tenkin* and those who did not want to. As a result, almost all female employees chose the latter, "area-based" jobs, acknowledging that their monthly salary would be 20,000 yen less. Only Ms. Watabe, the HR manager I interviewed, and very few others volunteered for the global category. Ms. Watabe mentioned her thought that many of them had to make that decision in their childrearing years. Ms. Watabe had also deliberated how to make her best choice. She had hesitated to talk about it in the workplace, so she called her friends and seniors who used to work for Hiroo and consulted with them on the phone. Eventually, she realized that she would want to be acknowledged as a career seeker. Then, she chose the global category.

Thus, the course-based hiring system is a sensitive issue that results in the gendered segregation of employment, as Lam (1992, 1993) argues. So, I was surprised when Mr. Satō at Okamoto Insurance showed me its work rules book that stipulates the requirements of *tenkin* and transfers as a matter of course. The rules said that all-area employees, who are in the top-career-track course of Okamoto Insurance Company, were required to accept *tenkin*. Regional-based employees were only required to accept transfers within a given locale, although it sometimes resulted in *tenkin* when the transfer necessitated a move of a domicile[5] but only when employees "consented" to it.

Mr. Satō put emphases on "consent" [*dōi*] which was written in the work rules book of area-based employees. This indicated two points. First, in Okamoto Insurance, transfer without a move of a residence was conducted flexibly for both all-area employees and regional-based employees. In implementation of transfers of these employees, no consent was necessary. Second, *tenkin* was conducted differently depending on the employee's category. All-area employees had *tenkin* in an unlimited manner. Area-based employees, on the other hand, could reject *tenkin* if they did not want it. As a result, employers felt that many female employees in this category had difficulties enhancing their skills, without transfers to other offices within the area. In other words, from the employers' viewpoint, these women end up in serving the same auxiliary job in the same office for a considerable number of years.

According to Mr. Satō's admittedly imperfect recollection, about five years ago, Okamoto Insurance implemented a personnel reform, in which the firm changed the naming of employment categories from career-track [*sōgōshoku*] and non-career-track [*ippanshoku*] workers to all-area [*zen-iki*] and area-based [*chiiki*] workers, respectively. It was for workers' "role innovation to enhance total productivity and reduce costs," according to Mr. Satō. For instance, auxiliary jobs that the non-career-track workers used to handle were taken by non-regular part-timers, or automated. For example, when people signed an insurance contract for their car, in the past, they might have made it on paper with an agent who explained everything verbally. The data they wrote on the paper was passed to another agent who stood by in the shop's back-office to input the data into a computer. Then it was sent to an administrative department in this head office, in which another clerk checked through everything again. If the clerk had found something wrong, she returned the contract to the shop and asked for correction. Nowadays, in these shops, tablet computers are employed for transactions, instead of paper. Their work became more and more streamlined. So, non-career-track workers had fewer things to do, unless they did planning jobs or sales jobs. All-area employees are required to develop new customers. That task is much harder and more time-consuming. But it can increase the revenue, that is, raise the profitability.

For these purposes, Okamoto Insurance reformed the personnel treatment of the area-based workers. It evaluated them "in the same ring in which all-area employees were treated," Mr. Satō said. This meant that in the personnel evaluations, regionally based employees became required to perform the same duties as all-area employees. For instance, the roles of a chief are the same, Mr. Satō remarked. "The difference between the two groups is whether he/she has nationwide *tenkin*."

But the inflexibility of *tenkin* for area-based employees had caused "discord," Mr. Satō mentioned. Without wide transfers including *tenkin*, area-based employees felt they could not fulfill the same roles as all-area employees. The firm had a large number of offices nationwide as well as worldwide, but area-based employees could not relocate. The posts where they could be sent at certain times of their career were not always available under the long-term employment system. Furthermore, some workers chose to stay in "clean" jobs, such as back-office work, and never attempted to challenge other jobs, such as sales, that often involved *tenkin*. Mr. Satō referred to this problem as "mismatch in demand-supply relations." As a result, transfers of area-based employees, mostly women, tended to be postponed. Ideally, they were transferred between positions every seven to eight years. But in practice, some workers had stayed in one post for almost ten years, which delayed their careers because they had experience in fewer positions overall in comparison to all-area employees, who had *tenkin* every five to six years because they were transferred more widely. With these differences in employment categories and consequent experiences, their roles to be evaluated could seldom be compared adequately.

Mr. Satō's comments about the area-based workers' inflexibility were critical. He insisted that these workers also accumulate a lot of job experience through *tenkin* and can compete with other workers. In this statement, he embodied the idea of Internal Labor Market that enables pricing and allocation of labor within the firm and exhibited a gendered double standard. While Okamoto Insurance had marginalized female employees in peripheral jobs across its history, the firm expected them to become actors in the labor market in recent years. This was clarified by Mr. Satō's remark that the inflexibility of the area-based workers had precluded his firm from enhancing women's employment. The ratio of the number of the female managers was 2 percent (Tōyō Keizai Shinpōsha 2014). He seemed to hope that if only the area-based employees changed their behavior in transfers, they could be promoted to managers. Interestingly, Mr. Satō did not question the fact that Okamoto had few women in all-area positions. For instance, the proportion of women who joined the firm as all-area workers was 6 percent in April 2015 (Tōyō Keizai Shinpōsha 2014), around the time of the interviews. Yet, he seemed to take it for granted, saying, "We always have more men in the all-area-worker category." By ignoring the gender inequality in the employment scheme, especially neglecting to question why it happened, the HR manager blamed female workers for clinging to area-based positions.

The gender gap was certainly caused by Okamoto's flexible implementation of *tenkin*. Mr. Satō specified his firm's other reasons for *tenkin* as promotion and rotation. First, the firm relocated the employees for promotion in position. Yet, such cases were rare in reality, because only a few positions such as chiefs, managers, and senior managers or executives were usually available, even if positions nationwide were taken into account. In the firm's seniority-based promotion system based on long-term employment, workers were promoted in rank, which is associated with small pay rises, but very seldom in position. Mr. Satō mentioned that there were many workers who ended their careers as managers but did not reach senior positions.

Thus, the employers took advantage of the written work rules and insisted on their control over the implementation of *tenkin*. When, why, how, and for how long the company required the workers to be transferred was not written, but served as the norm. Although Okamoto's work rules stipulated its workers' ability to reject a *tenkin* order with good reasons, the firm interpreted the regulation the other way around. As Mr. Satō said, "Our employees cannot reject *tenkin* without good reasons."

Without doubt, "good reasons" seemed not always granted. Okamoto Insurance actually set another purpose of *tenkin* as "private reasons." Mr. Satō called the practice "consideration [*hairyo*]," in which the firm took their workers' private conditions, or "good reasons," into account when they appointed *tenkin*. In practice, the firm provided online self-declaration sheets for the employees and let them state their career objectives, desires for the next job or place, and any private conditions they wanted the firm to recognize before any *tenkin* order. The request for a place can be met only when a post is available. But if there are other managerial factors, such as employees' personal situations to consider, the request can be granted. If one employee said, for instance, that he had a sick parent at home whom he had to take care of, and asked to move to a post near his house, the HR department would consider the request as much as possible, though not 100 percent. For another example, if an employee were still young, he might bring an issue about his child. Most such cases happened when children attended private schools.[6] But in these cases, the employees were transferred as a matter of course as *tanshin funin* [moving and living alone]. The firm will not forgo their *tenkin*.

For the employees to make the decision easier, the firm provides a "good *tanshin-funin* system," Mr. Satō insisted. As *tanshin-funin* allowance, first, transferees were paid about 100,000 yen for their immediate living expenses in new cities. That money could be used for necessities. They also received compensation for twelve or thirteen round-trips home (to visit their family). Also, in Okamoto, company housing [*shataku*] was provided, both for transferees and their families. Needless to say, their moving costs are paid, too. In case of accompanying family members as well, if a worker had to rent his house for someone, to supplement the loan of the house, the firm offered a service, called "relocation." This helped him find the renter. "We have such generous allowances for *tenkin*," he stated proudly. By this statement, it became clear that for the firm, maintaining their flexible *tenkin* structure usually outweighed considering workers' private conditions. The declaration system turned out to be a one-way request, just as in the firm's one-way stipulation of the requirement of *tenkin* in their work rules book.

Mr. Satō also mentioned that the firm continued to remind job-hunting students[7] that once they were employed as all-area workers, they would have to be ready for *tenkin* anytime and anywhere. Mr. Satō referred to their personnel system as a "structure that assumes *tenkin*" [*tenkin wo zentei to shita shikumi*]. Their statement about consideration was a façade. Behind the scene, their *tenkin* system that aimed to develop workers' careers, avoid possible crimes,[8] and also string them along, and thereby to meet the firm's business need, always outweighed any others under the hierarchical relations, although it caused the gender gap.

In Tachibana Newspaper, the possibilities of transfers after the training period usually decreased until the next time the employees requested them. Even though the possibility declined, and it was a request-based transfer, according to the managers, a certain norm of mandatory *tenkin* remains in the company, too. Mr. Kimura mentioned that Tachibana Newspaper provided a transfer request sheet [*idō kibō chōsa*] for their employees once a year. On the sheet, they were asked to declare where they wished to work. The sheet was open on the Intranet, the same as other firms, and regarded by those who had responsibility in the employees' personnel affairs and made decisions on transfers, usually HR managers. Mr. Kimura said that this practice had nothing to do with employees' evaluations. The company only asked their employees about their requests for transfers.

Yet in fact, the practice partly impacted promotion. When the workers were promoted in Tachibana Newspaper, before or at the promotion, they had to experience two different departments located in two different head offices, which resulted in *tenkin*. For example, for a writer, it could be *tenkin* from a news section in Tokyo head office to a political section in Osaka head office. For a sales person, it could be *tenkin* between two bureaus such as a sales office and an advertisement office between Osaka and Nagoya. In both cases, promotion could accompany at the time of the *tenkin* or after the *tenkin*. According to Mr. Kimura, workers tended to try to undergo the system in their thirties, so that they could show their engagement for their career to the HR department.

In practice, however, not all workers were provided with chances, as they desired. First, transfers, including those for promotion, depended on the availability of a post. Even if a worker volunteered for the challenge, if there was no position available for him to be able to cover, he had to wait for another chance. Under the long-term employment systems of Japanese firms, chances for promotions in positions were few. Second, if a worker was evaluated by her boss as better suited to another job, she might be transferred to that job, and not encouraged to challenge the promotion system. Although Mr. Kimura asserted that the transfer request system had no link with their evaluation system, it surely did so in this way. Furthermore, these practices revealed that the transfer request system for promotion ended up as one-way requests. Ultimately, the managers and HR department had the power to decide their workers' upward mobility in the personnel hierarchy. This practice was "stringing along."

Yet, the transfer request sheet actually played another important role. It could also function as a "no" request sheet, on which employees could declare that they did not wish for any transfers, and state their reasons. There was a box on the transfer request sheet in which the employees could reveal such private situations. When they had situations that they wanted the HR division to consider, they wrote them there and requested no transfer. Mr. Kimura described the practice as follows:

> Some people write about their private situations in great detail, but others not. For instance, I once saw one worker writing very specifically about his family structure, and describing how his family members need his help. For example, his parents have such and such diseases and necessitate his support for going to hospitals several times a week.

These days, female writers sometimes request "no" transfer coming back from local branches to the head offices, writing that they married and gave birth to their children in the cities, so they don't want to move from there for a while. "Because we have no rigid rules that our employees had to transfer at certain intervals, as banks usually do, we do not think staying in one position for long years is strange. That can happen."

But in reality, if she did so, it should mean that she gave up challenging the promotion system. There seemed to be a norm in Tachibana Newspaper that if workers wanted to seek careers, they were supposed to volunteer for transfers and prepare for them whenever the company requested.

As Mr. Kimura's comment implied, women of reproductive ages seemed to have more difficulty in going through the promotion system, than male employees. In fact, Mr. Tanaka mentioned that it was only around ten years ago that many of their local offices reformed the toilets from unisex to separate ones. The managers repeated several times that the ratio of women entering the firm as writers had been half recently. In order to retain these female workers, Tachibana adopted a reemployment system requested by its union in the year of our interview. The system called for re-hiring workers who had left Tachibana within five years for force majeure, such as *tenkin* of their husbands or childbirth. In addition, an increasing number of these female employees had stronger intentions than men for building their careers while enjoying private lives. They tended to submit the transfer request sheet to challenge the promotion system in their twenties, earlier than it used to be, based on their calculation about how the promotion system and their private life, including marriage and bearing and raising children, could be reconciled. The managers seemed to believe that these attempts would help the company increase the number of female managers gradually and the women responded to it. Yet, if *tenkin* remains being conducted by the firm's initiative during workers' reproductive periods, these aspirations, for both employers and employees, would be continuously obstructed. As a result of this, *tenkin* in Tachibana Newspaper, as well as in the other firms, was reproduced as gendered in contemporary Japan.

THE MALE-BREADWINNER MODEL AND *TENKIN*

The regulated, compulsory, purposeful, gendered practices of *tenkin* were regarded as natural so it was not rare that the practices penetrated into workers' private realms. Generally, given the male-breadwinner practices, workers ended up choosing one from two conventional choices: accompanying [*taidō*] or transferring alone [*tanshin funin*]. Both of them assumed gendered family formations and in turn brought a greatly gendered impact to workers' lives.

Accompanying

From my fieldwork, I could see that it the norm of wifely accompaniment was more robust than that of solo transfer. It was because of people's assumption based on the female-homemaker model that domestic roles should be fulfilled by women in their husbands' transferred places, as in Kurotani's (2005) book, *Home away from Home*. HR managers of the two firms here clarified that underpinning the norm of wifely accompaniment was a strong sense of seeking efficiency for the firm.

The practice of having workers be accompanied by family members in *tenkin* is called "accompanying family" [*kazoku taidō*]. Motomachi Manufacturing, the maker producing and selling electronic devices, clearly utilized this term. The firm's expectation and dependence on female domestic labor at their workers' transferred places was patently obvious. In response to my question about which they thought better, either their employees being accompanied by their family or moving alone to *tenkin*, Mr. Koyanagi remarked that it depended on the workers' family situations [*kazoku kankyō*] to begin with, and answered, "Of course, we prefer our workers to be accompanied by their family, if it is possible."

The vice president, Mr. Tsuchida immediately cut in, with an attempt to explain more. He mentioned children's education as the ground for the decision making. If their children have entrance exams or had already been enrolled in a school where those exams are required, the employees may (want the children to keep the educational advantages and) decide to move alone (to their *tenkin*). On the other hand, if their children are still very small, they may move all together. To the contrary, if their children are big enough to take care of themselves, they may have only their wives accompanying them. In the past, Motomachi encouraged its employees' families to accompany, with a belief that "it would allow the workers to devote themselves to their work in the transferred places, and also would help them to stay in good health." However, Mr. Tsuchida said, "nowadays, we understand that every worker has various individual issues in their private lives. So we entrust the workers themselves to decide, whether or not they accompany their family." Then, both Mr. Koyanagi and Mr. Tsuchida remarked that caring for elder parents seemed to be an urgent critical matter recently that had increasingly bothered their employees in their decision making. "If the elder care becomes a serious matter, more and more workers in Motomachi would choose *tanshin funin*," the managers said. By these statements, we learn that the managers may assume that any care, for both children and elder parents,[9] is the responsibility of their family, possibly women.

These practices rested on the male-breadwinner model. Behind both of the accompanying and *tanshin funin*, there was always the gendered assumption that women as wives of the corporate workers play caring roles at home, either overseas or in Japan. As the outcome, in Motomachi Manufacturing, men and women were usually divided into different employment categories, the career track and non-career track and the proportion of female managers was only 2 percent (Tōyō Keizai Shinpōsha 2014).

The gendered feature was actually seen throughout my visit to Motomachi. First, as soon as we got into the cozy drawing room for the interview, a female secretary dressed in a uniform immediately offered glasses of iced coffee to each of us. Both of the managers were gentle with benign smiles and they often tried to make me laugh with their answers with Kansai accents. Yet, they looked bothered at my questions about issues other than *tenkin*, such as women's activation [*Josei katsuyaku*], the governmental campaign held over the time of my fieldwork in 2015. It was perhaps because they thought it irrelevant to our interview about *tenkin* and also because they were not interested in talking about such issues at the first interview.

Yet, my follow-up interview in 2017, a year after the Act on the Promotion of Women's Active Engagement in Professional Life [*Josei katsuyaku suishin hō*] was enacted, revealed that the gendered norm in Motomachi seemed to be in transition. While the employers maintained the gendered division of the employment types, they hired an increasing number of highly educated women into the career track and made them experience *tenkin* and continue their jobs as wives and mothers. Through interactions with these new actors of *tenkin*, the employers needed to transform the practice to one not necessarily robustly relying on gender. I will elucidate this point in the next chapter.

Tanshin Funin

Solo transfer is the other family formation in *tenkin*. It was also taken for granted by many people I interviewed. It refers to *tenkin* of married workers who leave alone for their transferred place. The peculiarities of the practice in Japan were thoroughly addressed by Connor's (2010) study about public school teachers in Nagasaki Prefecture. The practice was originally derived from conventional gender patterns that women and men fulfilled separately in workplaces, families, and society.

The gendered expectation was manifested by the HR managers I interviewed. Ms. Watabe, at Hiroo Manufacturing, for example, indicated it from double viewpoints as the transferee and manager of the company. As noted earlier, the company carried out a personnel reform in 2002 and Ms. Watabe raised her hand for the global category. A few years before, she had *tenkin* as the first female employee of the firm. From this experience, she responded to my interview request through the company's online direct inquiry, she mentioned. That is, she had a personal interest in my research. At the time of her transfer, nearly ten years before the interview, Ms. Watabe was a married, forty-year-old mother with two daughters. Around the time when the younger daughter went to university, she was appointed to *tenkin* to a Tokyo office from the headquarters in Hiroshima Prefecture. It was a big surprise to her. Until that time, she had built her career in the field of information system development. By the *tenkin*, for the first time, she would handle jobs related to HR management. Actually, when she heard about the appointment a few months before that official announcement, she had hesitated to tell her family about it. She had been very aware that her husband would dislike her *tanshin funin*. She worried about her younger daughter, too. But she had not wanted to say "No" to the offer. Ms. Watabe knew that she had been selected for the first woman's *tanshin funin* in her company. Also, she recognized that her company had waited for the time, when her daughter had finished her entrance exam for university. In fact, Ms. Watabe had been asked her younger daughter's age by her boss numerous times every year. This practice that a company suspended female workers' *tenkin* until their children became university students seemed to be common among women in the forties and fifties. One of my informants, Ms. Nishino, a fifty-year-old career-track system engineer and manager, had the same experience in that she had asked her firm to wait for appointing her *tenkin* and subsequent *tanshin funin* until her daughter started to go to university. Ms. Nishino attributed the main reason for the holding to entrance exams of her daughter that had lasted until the daughter entered university. Up to that time, the mother, Ms. Nishino, had been responsible for her daughter's study and life overall.

In fact, Ms. Watabe had another practical reason for the acceptance. She was originally from Chiba Prefecture, therefore, she had hardly worried about going to and living in Tokyo, which is virtually next door. At last, she made up her mind to talk to her family, mainly her younger daughter, husband, and his mother who was already old at the time, but who lived nearby and promised to help out preparing meals for her granddaughter and son at their home. Contrary to her worries, her husband was supportive of her decision to accept *tenkin*. The husband encouraged her. Eventually, she was transferred to Tokyo for two and a half years and promoted to a managerial position. There, she herself was able to build a new network as a "new self," which was different from being a working mother in Hiroshima. Also, she had substantially changed her view toward the head office, mapping it from the outside. From this experience, Ms. Watabe, as the HR manager, held a view that a female employee could be the subject of *tenkin*, which was necessary for her HR development and promotion.

In Hiroo, the "global employment" scheme generally consisted of workers who graduated from university or above. Every year, around thirty-five global employees were hired and women accounted for around 19 percent on average between 2011 and 2016, a little more than the proportion of women of the whole employees, 17 percent, according to the company's website. In the other "area-based" scheme, female high-school graduates were hired on an irregular basis. The proportion of the female global employees was lower than male workers, because of three related reasons, according to Ms. Watabe. The first was the requirements for the global employees. The job was comprised of two categories: engineering, and sales and administration. The former deals with the development of the products, so all workers in the category were specialists. Since the ratio of female students who major in engineering in Japanese universities is small, 12.9 percent and 11.2 percent of undergraduate and graduate students, respectively (Gender Equality Bureau 2015, Figure I-6-4, Figure I-6-5), the proportion of female engineers was relatively small. Second, the latter office-based job did not attract women because it had *tenkin*. The job required a periodic *tenkin* for "appropriate personnel deployment [*tekisei na jinin haichi*]," according to Ms. Watabe. This implied compulsory relocation of those who could not show his/her best performance in sales. In such cases, the company tended to transfer their workers to other places in order to locate another worker who would earn more in the position. Third, furthermore, the job did not suit women. The sales job in Hiroo Manufacturing required the workers to drive a truck and carry heavy machines as their products to sell, as well as to maintain them. Listening to the description, women generally felt uneasy about taking responsibility for this job.

The gender-specific treatment for women was obvious in Hiroo's attitudes and strategies toward a "work-life balance." The company was well known for its efforts in its promotion. However, the subjects of the work-life balance strategy were always women. As one example published on its website, the female president encouraged their workers, particularly women, to have children, while they continued to work. To this end, Hiroo had promoted in-house marriage, so that the company could pay attention to and take care of female workers during their husbands' *tanshin funin*. Then, the female workers, backed up by the company, were supposed to "protect their family while rearing their children," according to Ms. Watabe. To make it possible, the company had also provided an in-house daycare center. In Hiroo Manufacturing, by addressing the gender division of labor and encouraging the workers to followit, the employers reinforced their legitimacy in pursuing efficiency under the gender-based personnel management.

Generally speaking, some Japanese companies seemed to think such in-house marriage caused trouble for women in cases of *tenkin*. This was because it would foster gender inequality not only in the practice of *tenkin* but also in their everyday workplaces. The companies prioritized male workers, and they sacrificed and marginalized their counterpart, female workers by putting family responsibility onto them. Indeed, this gendered personnel management recently caused a problem in Hiroo. Because the employers treated women in the global positions differently from male workers in the same position, exempting them from their requirement of *tenkin* during their childrearing period, the area-based female workers complained about the differences between their categories including their salary gap, saying, "Although they (global employees) also work for shorter hours as we do, and they will not have *tenkin* during the childcare period, why are they paid more than we are?" They, mostly the area-based employees in their forties or above who decided to stay in the category in the 2002 reform, had a strong feeling of inequality.

In response to such critiques, Hiroo Manufacturing adopted a new system two years ago. The global employees who were taking shorter working hours for childcare became required to have to change their employment category to the area-based. The shorter-hour system was allowed until their children become three years old. The global employees who had children under the age of three, and who took the shorter-hour system must change their category. Ms. Watabe thought this was good and remarked:

> If they stayed in the global category, they might have a lot to worry about, such as what they are going to do if they receive a *tenkin* order. Rather than that, during the time (in which the workers changed their job category to the area-based), they could devote themselves to childrearing, while getting accustomed to working after childbirth. Then, when their children reach three, they can apply for returning to the category. In this way, they have more sense of security.

Such uproars between the same genders commonly occurred in family-friendly companies such as Shiseido, as is well known as "Shiseido Shock"[10] (Tōyō Keizai Online 2016). The work-life-balance-oriented personnel treatment in the past has faced roadblocks in contemporary workplaces, where more and more workers are required to play pivotal roles and thereby take issues of fairness more seriously. By the adoption of the new system, Hiroo Manufacturing filled in the gap between the female employees, while the company deepened the one between the genders. In fact, there had been only one employee who had changed her category from the global to the area-based during her childbearing but soon later returned to her original category. Some workers in her department had been suspicious about her determination for *tenkin*. The employer had not sent her anywhere yet, but acknowledged her motivation and engagement in her career, as well as her commitment to the firm, Ms. Watabe said.

Recently, some female workers who had in-house marriages preferred following their husband's *tenkin* to *tanshin funin*. They tended to make the decision for their small children. In such growing cases, the company had tried its best to find a job for the accompanying spouse in her husband's transferred place and allowed her to work there as the area-based employee. In Hiroo, working mothers were treated as caregivers so this brought about tension among its female employees with regard to *tenkin* and the decision of their family formation.

In Kamisato Manufacturing, on the other hand, Ms. Meguro expressed another view on the family formation due to *tenkin*. She said, "I don't know the exact number, but I feel that living-apart marriage [*bekkyo-kon*] is very common here." Ms. Meguro had entered the company one year before the interview, moving from another firm. So, she had been able to compare the firm with her previous workplace and had been astonished by the fact that she had often heard the word, "living-apart marriage." For example, one employee told her, "Because we will have a baby soon, we have decided to live together for the first time (in their marriage after living-apart life due to *tenkin*)." Another employee, a manager in the forties, had returned from overseas and asked her one day, "What does marriage mean to us (in her living-together experience after her long-term separate living due to *tenkin*)?" These cases were seen not only in couples who both worked for Kamisato but also in couples in which one partner worked for Kamisato and the other worked for a different company. Mr. Kudō also agreed with the commonalities of the living-apart marriage. As Ms. Meguro clarified, the living-apart married couples around her were mostly between the twenties and forties, and perhaps childless couples. In their twenties, separate living, especially between in Japan and overseas, considerably affected their childbearing.

EFFICIENCY, CUSTOM, AND GENDER

We can see from the detailed accounts on *tenkin* by the HR people that *tenkin* embodies various purposes for the firms. All of them, part and parcel of the ILM, are conducive to the efficient running of firms in Japan. And people in the firms take this for granted.

The main purposes of *tenkin* are training and skill development. Through *tenkin*, workers are supposed to go through on-the-job training in the early stage of building their careers. Throughout the period, they develop their skills and narrow their specificity. This results in enabling employers to deploy the personnel to appropriate positions under long-term employment. In addition, written rules and unwritten customs help people take *tenkin* for granted. The HR manager, Mr. Satō at Okamoto Insurance, for example, emphasized the obligation of *tenkin* in their work rules book. He also mentioned various customary practices in their implementation of *tenkin*. Although the regulations of *tenkin* were favored by several court decisions, as I discussed in the

Introduction, and also stipulated by the government's model work rules book, they were only one-way promises by the firms. Thus, *tenkin* is efficient for firms, while it is mandatory for workers, even though no punishment was specified anywhere.

The gendered division of labor, as the force and effect of the ILM, allowed these firms to normalize the mandatory practices of *tenkin*. The HR managers at Hiroo Manufacturing indicated that employers limited family formations in *tenkin* by gender, either spouse or family-accompanying or solo transfer, which rested on assumptions of the gender division of labor at home and workplace. The category and the result can meet Ueno's (2009) theory of capitalism and patriarchy. The implementation of *tenkin* by contemporary Japanese firms is structurally reproduced by double layers of constraints by capitalists' logic and gendered family assumptions and their systems.

NOTES

1. It is not only Tachibana Newspaper but also other newspaper companies, according to my other informants and their corporate websites, that registered their main office [*honten*] in one city, Tokyo or Osaka, and called the other office as well as a few offices in other local cities such as Nagoya and Fukuoka as head offices [*honsha*]. It was due to their history that had developed and reproduced their organizational cultures and functions separately. For instance, many writers whom I interviewed, whichever company they belonged to, described their Osaka offices as "fond of news" [*jiken zuki*]. Also, they often mentioned that each head office had independent management control, particularly trainings for newly entering workers.

2. Literally, it is a practice in which an employer tells an employee in private what is going to be published about his/her personnel treatment later in an official announcement [*kōji*].

3. The term, *fūdo*, here can be interpreted with Tetsuro Watsuji's (1961) discussion. *Fūdo*, or a climate, "a means for man to discover himself" (Watsuji 1961: 8), is the space- and time-nature of subjective human existence developed through his individual and social mutual relationship, which can lead to culture (Watsuji 1961). The HR managers of Motomachi mentioned that their climate is workers' characteristics such as earnest [*majime*] or steady [*kenjitsu*], which were nurtured historically along with the development of their own business and that of their related companies.

4. This is usually called "regular personnel transfer" [*teiki jinji idō*], which tends to be conducted by many Japanese firms. This greatly bears on workers' lives. For instance, once the timing has passed without transfer orders, it means that they will compulsorily have to stay in the position and city for another year, even if they do not wish it. The particular time for the transfer is not necessarily April. One of my informants who worked for a railway company mentioned it is June in his cases, which has made him and other employees feel difficulty in accompanying their families to

the transferred place, as their children are made to change their school in the middle of the semesters.

5. This may cause confusion, as *tenkin* is inter-regional transfer. This type of *tenkin* refers to cases such as transfer from Kurihama in Kanagawa Prefecture to Kujukurihama in Chiba Prefecture. Both cities are beaches located within the Kantō region, but commuting between these cities takes more than three hours. So, in such cases, which rarely happen, a move of a residence is necessary and the transfer, even within the locale, becomes *tenkin*, only if the workers agree with it.

6. In Japanese compulsory school system, there are private and public schools for elementary and junior-high education. Students choose, apply for, and take exams for private school, so once they are enrolled in one private school, changing schools are systematically difficult. On the other hand, public elementary and junior-high schools generally only welcome students who live in their school district. Therefore, if they change their residences, they can and also need to change the schools.

7. Job hunting [*shūshoku katsudō*] or its abbreviation [*shūkatsu*] is students' first and easiest access to jobs, or companies, in Japan, as Gordon Mathews (2004) describes. It is a collective event lasting for several months, through which college students, generally the fourth-grade, take an advantage of it before their expected graduation. During the event, the students are asked to visit companies' seminar, write a numerous number of CVs, called "entry sheet," and take steps of interviews.

8. This practice was often heard in financial industries such as banking and insurance business, but also in financial and accounting divisions of corporations I interviewed. People tend to believe that the longer a person serves in a certain job, the more likely the person is to commit white-collar crimes.

9. Due to the increase in longevity and the rise of women working throughout their lifetimes, eldercare has become a pressing matter for Japanese workers. For the issue, the Motomachi manager mentioned that automation, of which the company had invested in the development, would be one good solution. In the meantime, more and more people have become suffering from double care (Soma and Yamashita 2020). The care issues will be increasingly serious in aging Japan.

10. In 2015, NHK featured a personnel change of a cosmetic company in a morning news program. The manufacturer, well known as family friendly, had provided multiple work-life balance policies for its female employees, such as long-term childcare leave and a shorter-hour working system. But, this had caused friction between those who were eligible for the policies and those who were not. After a series of discussions, in 2013, the HR department of the company decided to treat both parties as fair as possible and began to ask the working mothers to try to work in the same conditions as other workers. Since such a decision was made by the top family-friendly company, it was regarded as a "shock."

Chapter 2

Development and Changes in the Practice?

Some multi-national manufacturers had sought to change their ways of implementation over time, as Kamisato Manufacturing in chapter 1 indicated. The company unions and working groups of employees attempted to fluctuate the ground of *tenkin*. Their purpose for the actions were to balance their work and family lives. The interviews I conducted in 2017 revealed these firms' efforts. From these actions, it seemed that the practice of *tenkin* was at crossroads.

Yet, analyzing it through the lenses of gender, their assumptions and ensuing systems that they provided for employees commonly continued to rest on the breadwinner model. Some employers assumed, without doubt, their married employees to move together all along to the transferees' *tenkin*. These cases relied on someone of the family members, often simply a wife, for domestic household and care labor. To put it differently, there was little idea that both of the couples build and manage twin careers through *tenkin*. In the same logic, there was little effort to be made for reconsidering the practice of *tenkin* itself. In this way, the practices of *tenkin* were reproduced as cultured and gendered by the large firms in contemporary Japan.

ATTEMPTS TO RECONSIDER EMPLOYMENT SYSTEMS AND *TENKIN*

Some of the firms, manufacturers in particular, remarked that they are required to catch up with the global business. The three interviews I conducted in February 2017 with Motomachi, Mizuki, and Satomura revealed that two of them had carried out the reconsideration of their practices of *tenkin* and the practices-related systems. The ground for the reconsideration came from the concept, "diversity and inclusion," of which I heard not only in my interviews but also in the events I participated in. Initiated by foreign companies, the term served as an icon for firms who were tackling rigorous employment management and trying to adapt to something new. In respect of *tenkin*, it meant inclusion of diverse actors, first, female employees to subjects of *tenkin*, and second, wives of transferees to secured employees even if their husbands had *tenkin*. By these attempts, such firms hoped to increase female managers and meet the requirement of the Act on the Promotion of Women's Active Engagement in Professional Life, while not radically reconsidering the gendered practice of *tenkin*.

Reforms of *Tenkin*-Related Practices

Mizuki Manufacturing, where I interviewed in February 2017, strove to seek better solutions in its personnel system for the sake of its business across history. Mizuki Manufacturing was a lingerie maker and 88 percent of its roughly 5,000 regular employees were women. However, the proportion of female managers was far less, 21 percent. The firm therefore attempted to conduct a reform to increase female managers in such a gendered workplace, expecting them to play more proactive roles in its increasingly global business.

As a lingerie manufacturer, Mizuki had a number of special workers [*senmonshoku*], who were in charge of sales, designs, and laboratory research. According to an HR manager, Ms. Tachi, they were also called "limited workers" [*gentei shoku*] because they only specialized in a certain job and also work in a certain area, and they were not required to do nationwide *tenkin*. Because of these limitations, the employees in this category were almost all women, and they were seldom interested in promotion, Ms. Tachi remarked. These women tended to think that promotion and becoming managers was a story of another island. It was partly because they were treated as women. For instance, when Ms. Tachi had gone to Europe for business more than a decade before, she had to take a male employee as a "knight," even though she did not need one. She said, "He later told me that, thanks to me, he was able to travel overseas" [laugh]. Ms. Tachi added:

> Our company had tended to treat women as little girls and women also made their minds as such. Male managers had been well trained to take care of these women and women had been happy and comfortable with that. So, these male managers were preferred by the women, as female managers were more strict with women, of the same gender.

Therefore, most of the managers were men, who were promoted from the career track. Because promotion required nationwide *tenkin*, according to another manager, Mr. Higashi, fewer women were in this category. For example, around twenty years before, Mizuki welcomed seventeen new career-track workers in total, and only two of them were women, although it increased the number recently. In 2016, a little more than half of the total thirty career-track employees were women. The firm used to be a highly gendered workplace and had attempted to change it.

An initiative for the change was led by the president, a few years before and Ms. Tachi was one of the project leaders. She had thought it problematic for many years that many of the female workers, mostly in the special jobs, had not volunteered to become managers, or rather, they had ostensibly depended too much on others in the responsibility of the management. On the other hand, the firm's research had shown that 70 percent of the male career-track workers had tended to prefer to become managers, regardless of their abilities. But, Ms. Tachi had also interpreted this situation that this difference itself had indicated scores of their abilities. More precisely, "The fact that men could be able to image their career very positively was an ability," she added. Given the reality, the project team had been established. First, the team had sent a message that women themselves were the subjects who were involved in the management of our company. Then a series of voluntary training programs were held for women so that they could learn about leadership. The project was successful in that women, who were in their prime time to be managers, changed their minds to show more interests in boosting their careers. As a result, the proportion of the female managers rose from 10 to 20 percent. In addition, other women, who were not yet of managerial age, were also stimulated. Furthermore, Mizuki realized that the inclusion of the specialists into the generalists, which was a main project in the reform, was likely to contribute to diversification of the management and thereby to innovation in the business.

However, the project was far from completion. Mizuki Manufacturing was still behind in the number of female career-track workers who were in managerial positions, the same as other Japanese firms. Since Mizuki had hired fewer women in its career-track job for many years, in its seniority-based promotion system, the company still had to wait for another few years to promote female career-track employees. Another HR staff, Ms. Sudō, a career-track employee and mother of three children, would be one of them. As a mother whose youngest child was one-and-a-half years old, she tried to manage her childcare and responsibilities as a career-track worker.

Like Ms. Tachi, the other HR manager, Mr. Higashi attributed the gender gap of the career-track workers also to the issues of subjectivities. According to Mr. Higashi, career-track employees were supposed to do their jobs of their own accord. To this end, the firm provided a rotation for them, which could involve *tenkin*, regardless of the workers' will. The rotation aimed for their business to function well. There used to be an era when some highly specialized workers could play their roles in their responsible jobs and the company functioned as a whole. "But nowadays, when the company is facing roadblocks in enhancing their business, they need fresh air," Mr. Higashi said. They need a person from another field with a different specialty, who can see a problem from a different angle with a fresh mind and knowledge. Mr. Higashi added, "In a typical Japanese company like ours, we always feel fettered by relationships between people and tend to have difficulties in posing our opinions." This is the ground for Mizuki to conduct *tenkin*. That is, the workers need to be assigned to a position to which they have barely aspired and expected to bring fresh ideas and energy to the new post and find good solutions. Asking for a proactive attitude toward a compulsory practice seemed inconsistent, but in their own logic, it was legitimate.

Not only in the mandatory transfers but also in their daily jobs, the workers in Mizuki were expected to pro-actively negotiate the boundaries of their jobs. As a "typical Japanese company," as Mr. Higashi repeated, the workers were not provided any job descriptions. In other words, their assignments were not determined by anyone. This condition is consistent with Cole's (1979) finding I addressed above that Japanese workplaces tend to lack sharp jurisdictional definitions of job duties and both management and workers tend to make Japanese workers less conscious of job changes. So, the company expected the workers to do what, how, and why subjectively, and they believed that it would contribute to their own career development. "Unless they tried to find prospects in their jobs, it's not likely that their careers would develop. So if we see someone always complaining about not being given any chances, we tend to ask him/her, 'Have you told anyone that YOU want a challenge?' although it is not enough to change their mind," Mr. Higashi mentioned. In Mizuki, the proactive attitudes meant negotiation of workers in themselves and with others.

However, such attitudes eventually seemed to have brought change to the practice of overseas mandatory *tenkin*. Mizuki Manufacturing had factories overseas, in which the products were made. The firm had sent its career-track workers to the sites to manage local staff hired by a joint venture. This resulted in *tenkin* overseas. In this practice of *tenkin*, Mizuki's HR division had chosen transferees until recently, rather than asking for volunteers. So, Ms. Tachi mentioned that she knew one worker who had kept banging his head on a wall over and over every night in a hotel where he had stayed, crying over his poor language and communication skills in a local factory. Even in such cases, the *tenkin* was not withdrawn. But lately, Mizuki was trying to transform the practice, in overseas cases in particular, to one that relied more on workers' proactive attitudes in the long run. The company used to send their employees to overseas sites as managers when they were in the late thirties or over forty years old. Recently, however, it had tried to let younger workers take a chance in their twenties, especially the technicians, or around thirty years old for others. They were also selected. This was because, Mr. Higashi believed, the *tenkin* aims to allow them not merely to experience life and work overseas, but rather to learn about the management. So, even if they were good at language, if they would not manage the local staff, it would be nonsense. One of his co-workers in its international division told him that "passion" and "never-give-up spirit" were getting more important to succeed the management overseas. Therefore, the company came to prioritize humanity (and select an employee with such character).

However, in terms of the language, the firm was trying to establish a program, in which its workers would study abroad and improve their language and communication skills in their early thirties, after they developed their business skills in Mizuki. This would help to develop both of their skills. And the challenge would be voluntary. This change is because, Mr. Higashi said, its employers had, at last, realized that sending employees who only have humanity but barely spoke the language had ended up in failure, after all, in management overseas.

The new practice of voluntary transfer, to study abroad, would be implemented through negotiation by its employees. By pushing the practices of proactive attitudes and negotiation, Mizuki Manufacturing was changing the cultural normative practice of *tenkin* to the one negotiable. With the new practice, the firm's female workers would be the subjects, too, while *tenkin* was still tied to the training, skill specificity, and custom.

Diversity and Inclusion Projects

Motomachi Manufacturing, the manufacturer of electronic parts which believed that the transfers are the climate [*fūdo*], brought a change to gender-unequal culture recently. The company adapted to the social movement for women's advancement. My follow-up interview in 2017 revealed that the HR managers, Mr. Tsuchida and Mr. Ueda, increasingly saw their women's employment situations as problematic, particularly the job continuity of the female workers and also their low proportions in managerial positions. The company then set up a project seeking "diversity and inclusion for better innovation." As one policy, Motomachi adopted a new target for recruiting more female workers, 10 percent for career-track technicians and 40 percent for sales and administrative career-track workers. The target figure of the technicians was smaller, as Mr. Tsuchida mentioned, because the ratios of the female students who major in engineering in Japanese universities are smaller than that in humanities and social sciences. Around the time of the interview, they consisted of 12.9 percent and 11.2 percent of undergraduate and graduate students, respectively (Gender Equality Bureau 2015). The company expected to raise the women's employment rate up to the social average.

This process unveiled that the company was considerably male dominated. As for women's greater advancement to managerial positions, pushed by the 2016 Act on the Promotion of Women's Active Engagement in Professional Life, the firm did not attempt any strategies. They explained that when they had actually mentioned the attempt in front of their employees, their male workers opposed it, saying, "Why only women?" So, the HR members decided to establish the concept of "inclusion" first and then seek the next step in the strategy, so that these male workers would not pose questions about fairness and equity. Apparently, men had "voices" (Schoppa 2006), while women did not.

Yet, the series of efforts by the employers resulted in contributing to promoting career-track female workers, including Ms. Hino, whom I describe in a later chapter. In the diversity and inclusion project, Motomachi Manufacturing built a new practice, called the spousal following leave system [*haigūsha dōkō kyūgyō seido*]. It allowed their workers to follow their spouses' *tenkin* overseas by taking a three-year leave. Mr. Tsuchida admitted that the adoption of the system had been bargained by their company union and a young study group voluntarily organized around the time in the course of their diversity and inclusion reform. The main purpose for the adaption was to retain their female workers and let them commit more to their own career development in Motomachi. The result was, to the contrary, that it helped the male worker, Ms. Hino's husband, take and live overseas together as a family. The negotiable workplace culture produced the less-gendered outcome in this case.

With these actions of Motomachi Manufacturing across history, an issue of fairness should be discussed in Japanese workplaces. The meaning of fairness was cultural. In most of the Japanese workplaces that I studied, it meant "the same" treatment. If someone was treated differently from the workplace norm, it was unfair. One condition was whether that someone was in the same employment category or not. In other words, if that someone was in a different category, for example, in which he/she earned less, even if he/she was treated worse, fairness did not matter. To the contrary, if he/she in such a different category was treated better or as special, fairness matters, as my individual informants including Mr. Hayashi in chapter 3 exhibited deep irritation. Fairness in Japanese workplaces meant that workers in the same category had to be treated in the same way, in terms of working conditions and ways of promotions, under the basic system of seniority-based pay and long-term employment. There is little sense of equity here. To this end, *tenkin* tended to be conducted mandatorily and periodically for career-track employment of Japanese firms, and the implementations were taken for granted in the society.

The male workers of Motomachi Manufacturing seemed to have raised this point. Since these men noticed that women in the same employment category would be treated differently, they saw it problematic from their senses of "fairness." The HR managers actually mentioned this word several times during our interview, when they explained their ways of promotion in relation to *tenkin*. Mr. Tsuchida remarked:

> We put great efforts into our promotion system. In addition to appraisals, we have writing tests and interviews for career-track employees. We take fairness [*kōhei*] and justice [*kōsei*] seriously, although I can't say whether it is good or not. Moreover, when our workers are promoted to managerial positions, they are evaluated by another firm, to which we entrust further assessment of them. The whole process is strict, I think.

Promotion should be usually visible by physical transfers of workers including *tenkin*. The HR managers therefore required to fill in the gap of the differences caused by promotion. For this purpose, the firm entailed interpersonal negotiation and attempted to raise their workers' senses of understanding in any personnel treatment. By doing so, Motomachi attempted to integrate female workers as main actors in the practice of transfers, aiming to succeed in the global business. Their employment practices seemed to be in transition, but still again, the factors of the ILM such as training, skill specificity, and custom, were present, and so was the gendered workplace.

TENKIN AT THE CROSSROADS

The firms, such as Mizuki Manufacturing and Motomachi Manufacturing, which attempted to lead change in their HR management including *tenkin* were distinctive from those who did not. First, the series of reforms were initiated by employees themselves, including the company union and working groups. The workers seemed to exert agencies individually and collectively. This helped the employers review the effects of *tenkin*, and thereby, the practice of *tenkin* itself. Second, the reforms aimed at diversity and inclusion. More specifically, the employers at both Mizuki and Motomachi were aware that the more female workers they attempted to include in managerial positions, the more diversified the workplace became, and the more innovative ideas the companies could pursue in their global competitions. The idea of fresh air was embodied in their management, even if the initiative was led by the 2016 enactment of the Act on the Promotion of Women's Active

Engagement in Professional Life. Third, in these workplaces, they pushed building negotiable labor-management relations forward. They found that the one-way practices of considering and being considered did not stimulate the workers to construct their subjectivities. Rather, they learned the importance of mutual communication in their everyday workplaces, to raise understanding with people from diverse backgrounds, although the practice ended up being held in the hierarchy, between employers and employees.

Behind these personnel changes, there was the impact of the global economy. Lately, since these manufacturers were required to compete in the severe global business environment, they needed to make their workers play active roles in it, by making full use of their job skills, languages, as well as human capabilities. In this context, their changes might be also driven by the larger economic force.

What happened as a result was that both firms still had difficulties in getting rid of gendered boundaries on their own and completely incorporating the female workers who had family responsibility into managerial positions. Through the processes, indeed, various tensions arose one after another, between genders or within one gender. Legal statutes and negotiation were insufficient to transform firms toward a gender-equal model. These follow-up interviews I conducted in 2017 clarified that *tenkin* is thus firmly embedded still in Japan's contemporary employment structure.

Then how do the employees react their firms' practices of *tenkin*?

Chapter 3

Young Workers and *Salariiman*

From this chapter, I will elucidate individual workers' stories of *tenkin*. They include their own *tenkin* experience and that of their spouses, or both, depending on their jobs and the length of their careers.

One similarity in their experience is that almost all of the workers tended to take the practice of *tenkin* for granted. Some echoed the purposes of *tenkin* that the HR managers mentioned, one of which was career development. These workers seemed to have constructed their senses of the practice ever since they entered their companies. Then they were accustomed to building careers and making better lives with *tenkin*. In their workplaces, they attempted to take advantage of *tenkin* at every turn. These responses demonstrated how powerful the market's logic of efficiency is and how robust the gendered structures are in contemporary Japan.

IN THE EARLY STAGE OF CAREER DEVELOPMENT

More male workers than female workers who had experienced their own *tenkin*, whom I encountered during my fieldwork, took their requirement of *tenkin* for granted. When I posed them several questions about *tenkin*, they looked baffled, or as if they saw somebody odd, although some people curiously asked why I became interested in it. I explained to them my own experience that I myself had had several experiences of *tenkin* while I had worked for a private company and often questioned about the practice. A majority of them responded to me that as career-track employees, they were supposed to accept *tenkin* orders, and therefore, even though they had difficulty in their private lives on account of it, for example, in living alone and eating simple meals alone, that was their problems, not their employers'. Accepting *tenkin* was common sense in their consciousness and attitudes, just as they allowed their work to penetrate their private lives.

The consciousness of taking *tenkin* for granted was most strongly embedded into the workers in the early stages of their career building including job-hunting periods. It was first because, as I discussed in the Introduction based on the previous research, during the time actors were single or childless so that they could accept the requirement of the practice without being bothered by work-life balance.

Dreaming of Overseas *Tenkin*

Moreover, since *tenkin* is often associated with living abroad, job-hunting students whom I observed in Waseda University ambitiously wanted to know if they would have a chance for *tenkin* overseas. They posed questions, for instance, what kinds of workers had such chances and how often did such transfer occur? In order to obtain the opportunities, what did the workers need to prepare while they were students? In so doing, they preferred to use the word, *chūzai*, rather than *tenkin*. The term is an abbreviation of *kaigai chūzai*, which literally means staying overseas. Since the time of high-speed economic growth, this term had been a symbol of a winner in career competitions, as Kurotani (2005) depicted. It represented challenges not only in one's career but also in one's family life. Also, it implied an economic benefit for the family, because people tended to believe that one overseas *tenkin* experience would provide the family with a comfortable allowance so as for them to be able to build a house in their home country eventually. All in all, *tenkin* overseas was viewed positively by the young people I met during the fieldwork.

In contrast to their enthusiasm for foreign *tenkin*, the students rarely asked about domestic *tenkin*. Although there were employees in the job-hunting event who worked for manufacturers based in Osaka and Fukuoka, the students had no interest in asking about possible moves of residence between these cities. This behavior indicated that domestic *tenkin* might be relatively seen as taken-for-granted, or, it might be completely ignored by the students. Both attitudes seemed to have been correlated in the respect that the students in the session were not afraid of the possibilities of *tenkin*. This may be because they believed that they would be able to go along with the practice, as contemporary society appeared to be friendly to working women and working parents. The students seemed to envision their careers and private lives as full of prospects. They were not much conscious of the gender and compulsoriness surrounding the practice of *tenkin* or in the workplace at large.

Playing *Salariiman*

Japanese white-collar workers, or *sarariimen,* are often said to be willing to show engagement and commitment to their employers, as I discussed in Introduction. Behind them, there are women in the domestic sphere who are required and willing to fulfill their family roles (Kurotani 2005). Such gendered attitudes were occasionally seen in *tenkin* for dual-career couples as well. No matter how hard their wives work in both workplaces and homes, *sarariimen* foist family responsibilities onto their working wives.

The most common practice for these male workers was that they were ordered for *tenkin* and they accepted it. Their employers, usually their bosses, dictate the male workers to move the positions. The workers, even if questioning the order, did not resist it.

Mr. Hayashi, a thirty-nine-year-old career-track male worker at a railway company was typical. He had a number of experiences of transfers including two times of *tenkin*, and every time, the transfers were ordered. His company was based in Osaka Prefecture, where he had been born and raised until he moved to Tokyo to attend university. Mr. Hayashi entered his company because he was interested in a planning job in real estate. For his initial five years in his company, therefore, he had developed his career in planning the development of real estate situated around stations on the railway line.

However, at his fourth assignment, he was suddenly and unexpectedly transferred to a department handling the development of the stations per se, not the surrounding real estate, and his job became coordination, not planning, of various related parties in the operation. Since then, for over ten years, Mr. Hayashi had been bound to this specialization against his wish. At the time of the interview, he told me, "I have no idea of what brought me to my current position, which is totally irrelevant in respect to my previous career." Moreover, for that career, he had *tenkin* twice. First, he had been sent to the Ministry of Land, Infrastructure, and Transportation in Kasumigaseki, Tokyo, for two years. It was a bolt from the blue. He had even never heard of that job before. In his knowledge, he mentioned, an external factor had worked for this assignment. In the first place, Mr. Hayashi had few co-workers who had entered his firm in the same year due to the long-lasting stagnation after the collapse of the bubble economy at the time. When Mr. Hayashi was transferred to the ministry, most of his few co-workers had handled local jobs as trainees and they had coincidently been pivotal manpower in these local offices. For the HR department to move them from these positions was unfeasible. Only Mr. Hayashi by chance had worked in the head office at the time and thereby had become the only candidate for *tenkin*. He was told by his boss, "I don't think you are the best person, but there is no one else (available for the transfer). Whether you may agree or not, just go. I don't know if this transfer will contribute to your career, but we have to send somebody. Please have fun in Tokyo." After all, he spent two years in Tokyo with his newly married wife. When he had his next regular transfer order, he came back to Osaka, with a promotion in rank.

When four years passed, Mr. Hayashi received another order of *tenkin*, to the Chūgoku area that time. At the second *tenkin*, again, he was the only candidate. His boss mentioned, "Nothing we can do. If you feel bitter, blame the time you live in (in which few workers had been employed and there were no other candidates than him)." Thus, Mr. Hayashi barely had any feelings of being "selected" for all the transfers and *tenkin* during those years.

Despite his unhappiness, Mr. Hayashi had seldom attempted to decline the orders of transfers and *tenkin*. When I asked about it, he merely responded, "I can't . . . I cannot say 'No, because it is a horizontal transfer,' can I? Or, can you?" [laugh]. As he had experienced many times, his firm transferred its career-track workers periodically, every two to three years. This generated transfers without promotion. He explained the reasons for the frequent moves as "remains from the era when we were managed by the state [*yakusho no nagori*]." Mr. Hayashi's company was privatized thirty years ago. As shown in the experiences of my other informants below, the national government had a practice of periodical transfers including *tenkin*. But, Mr. Hayashi remarked, "Only if we had family situations [*kateino jijō*] (might I have said 'no' to my *tenkin* orders)." As I noted above, Article 26 of the revised Child and Family Care Leave Law (MHLW 2010) could be the ground for workers to evade their transfer orders in Mr. Hayashi's company.

But, his "only if" had never materialized. Even though he himself had such "family situations" as a father of two children, a seven-year-old daughter and three-year-old son, he had never challenged his *tenkin* orders. It was clear when he had the second sudden *tenkin* to Hiroshima, and when his wife was pregnant with her second child, suffering from serious morning sickness every day. She had even been hospitalized and thereby the couple had needed support in housework from Ms. Hayashi's mother who had to come over by bullet train. Moreover, it was when the family had just started living in a brand-new house that they had bought. He mentioned:

If I were a married woman, my wish to stay in Osaka for this situation could be granted. However, a situation such as "I have a child and I bought a house" applies to everybody else, too, right? I think what has happened to me is also what is happening to workers in other companies, too. Moreover, when we are in higher ranks in seniority, available posts will decrease and the company would have difficulty in rotating these employees as fairly as possible. So in my *tenkin* to Hiroshima, I was only told "Good luck!"

Mr. Hayashi behaved like a good worker in the company on one hand, and he complained about his company's treatment of female career-track workers. In these narratives, he displayed his gendered view. He had heard about a case in which his company had taken the female workers' family situations into consideration [*hairyo*], held back their *tenkin* orders, and sent somebody else to the position instead. He believed that mothers were allowed to influence the personnel decisions, or the company. He said:

> Being a mother is like having a family crest [*mondokoro*].[1] These days, everyone says that we should raise children together and make the workplace family-friendly. So, mothers are more and more protected. If men did the same way, we would be seen as selfish. Our voices (of complaining about its unfairness) would be no bigger than our grumbles in a bar. My male friends working at manufacturers also complain about the women's special treatment, saying, "They (the female workers) must go to Asia, too. Otherwise, they should not present them in magazines as a career woman!" [laugh] I wonder, how come they are promoted, without *dosa mawari*,[2] only keeping themselves comfortable and warm in the head office.

He showed double standards. On one hand, he said "only if," but on the other hand, he thought the treatment unacceptable. For him, again, accepting nationwide *tenkin* had to be common sense for workers who seek promotion. Those who had limitations for *tenkin* should not be evaluated.

Nonetheless, Mr. Hayashi had never imagined working mothers' *tenkin* in a real situation. When I asked him for his opinion about why children are always with mothers, not fathers, in a case of *tenkin*, he could barely come up with any good reasons. I questioned him further if he had imagined it in his own case. He answered that it had been impossible practically, and he had never thought about it in his life. Then he added that it would be feasible only if his children became high-school students because for him, it was impossible to finish his work early and go pick up his children from a daycare center or after-school. Besides, he had never heard of such cases in his offices, either, in which men are primary caregivers for their children. In the interview, though, he was trying to think about why he thought so and others did so, too. He told me, "Maybe the women do not want to leave their children in their husbands' care. It may be a stereotype, though." Finally, he said, "If they (the gender roles in both workplace and home) became equal, our grumbles in the bar might disappear."

The cultural, gendered practice of *tenkin*, was clearly addressed by Mr. Hayashi. His firm was male dominated in all respects, such as the number of female workers, the personnel treatment, and the consciousness and attitudes of the workers. This largely affected Mr. Hayashi's behavior. He regarded seeking career advance and putting domestic responsibilities onto women as a perfect match. Even as a dual-career couple, he reproduced the *sarariiman* model.

Some male informants, who also played *salariiman* in terms that they did not question any conflicts occurring between their roles in *tenkin* and in private life, shared positive experiences and views of *tenkin*. For example, Mr. Kaji, a thirty-five-year-old career-track employee at one of the biggest general insurance companies, was most positive. He was from Saitama Prefecture and lived there with his parents until he graduated from university. He disliked, "only knowing about the Kantō area." During job-hunting, therefore, he looked for a job that required and allowed him to move and live in cities other than the area. He encountered a career-track job in a general insurance company. At a personnel interview to decide his first assignment before entering the company, he actually requested HR managers to send him as far away as they could. Although he meant *tenkin* to the northern area, including the Tohoku area and Hokkaido Island, the result turned out to be *tenkin* to Kagoshima Prefecture, at the completely opposite end of the main island. Mr. Kaji told me this episode with a laugh.

In his company, *tenkin* was mandatory for career-track employees, the same as in Okamoto Insurance. His firm did not listen to his request for places. So whichever places he requested or would request the HR division to send him to, it would rarely be reflected in his actual transfer. He thought that in asking him his preferences, the HR department was trying to ascertain his career goals. However, his wishes were not always taken into account. They, not he, decided where the workers go.

He said that he had not felt badly about this practice. He entered the firm, knowing that the firm had *tenkin* and he would accept the order wherever he would be sent. He thought that his *tenkin* was decided when one post became vacant and needed to be filled. Most of the time, one *tenkin* led to another. Also, he had the possibility of *tenkin* every month, although he knew that other general insurance firms did it once or twice a year. When he had *tenkin* to Ishikawa Prefecture (from Kagoshima Prefecture), there was no pre-announcement. One day, all of a sudden, he was told by his boss that he would have *tenkin* the following month. He moved as the company ordered. When he arrived at his new office in Ishikawa Prefecture, he found that someone had resigned from the job there and the company needed to fill the position by sending someone from somewhere. That someone was Mr. Kaji. Then the position in Kagoshima was filled by another person. This practice of *tenkin* seems to be the same as the one in Okamoto Insurance.

When he was sent to the Chūgoku area (where he worked at the time of our interview), it was sudden, too. He was told by his boss during their lunch time, while they were eating Chinese noodles together. He found out later that the Hiroshima office was reorganized and they needed more workers, and in

Ishikawa, he was the oldest employee in terms of the length of the transfer period. So, he was nominated. By that time, he had been in the position for almost four years. Usually, they had *tenkin* every three to five years.

Then, Mr. Kaji echoed the purpose of *tenkin*, which was similar to the one addressed by Okamoto Insurance:

> I am not sure if it is only (the practice) for financial industries, but if you stayed in one post for many years, you would have more risk of committing collusion by *yuchaku*. I think avoiding this risk is the major purpose (for *tenkin*). In fact, I myself feel it in the same way. The longer I stay in one position, the less I am pressured, because the relationship is less and less tense. In other words, I can imagine that under such too close and too long relationships, people easily overlook what they are supposed to notice, ask, and hear. Since our company deals with money, we do our best to avoid such cases (by moving personnel periodically).

Whether it is really effective or not, he gave full understanding to the practice also from his own experience.

This response toward *tenkin* was correlated not only with his aspiration to live in cities away from the Kantō area but also with the actual experience that he acquired from living in various cities. Mr. Kaji described the experience as "enriching my life." It meant that the more communities and people he knew, the stronger he could be when he would be faced with different viewpoints or values in his life. He said his wife thought that, too, and the life was worth living that way. His wife, Ms. Kaji was present at the interview. Listening to this, she was nodding next to him, showing how much she agreed with his opinion. For this purpose, the couple often traveled around the world. The couple only showed a little ambivalence when they started to talk about their expecting new life with a child. At the time of the couple's interview, Ms. Kaji was pregnant. Ms. Kaji, who used to experience her father's frequent *tenkin* in her childhood, grew to question how enjoying *tenkin* would affect their daughter. Ms. Kaji had a full-time job while her mother did not. Yet, the couple still had time to consider until the child is born. When I asked their opinion about the opposite case that some people absolutely wanted to stay in one place for their whole life, the couple answered, with a little sound of contempt, that they had been actually wondering what other people thought. Mr. Kaji thus regarded *tenkin* as precious for his life.

These ways, there were many types of *tenkin*, depending on workers' jobs, specialty, and industry. Another male worker, Mr. Takahara, a thirty-six-year-old national government official, showed another different experience. At the time of the interview with him, Mr. Takahara was based in Tokyo. However, his original affiliation the Chūgoku region[3] which included Okayama, Hiroshima, Yamaguchi, Shimane, and Tottori Prefectures. Mr. Takahara had chosen the area because he was originally from Yamaguchi Prefecture and he had wanted to contribute to the region in which he grew up. Actually, he had challenged a test for local government officials of the prefectures in that area, but it was "not successful," he said. Right after he began his job as a national government official in the Chūgoku area, he had in fact worked in the Hiroshima office for two years. After that, at the time of a periodic transfer, he had *tenkin* to Tokyo upon his request. Then after he married his wife, who worked for a general insurance company in Tokyo, he received a *tenkin* order to Hiroshima four years. During the appointment, Mr. Takahara moved to Osaka to study at a graduate school for two years. Mr. Takahara explained the back-and-forth transfer systems as the taken-for-granted stance. As a national government official, they are required to move between departments every two to three years to build a network to work more efficiently. He said, "If I work with someone I have known better, I can speak to the person without worrying too much about how much knowledge he/she has. Such cases help us do our jobs smoothly, and also, let us come up with a new idea."

In the decisions of *tenkin*, Mr. Takahara said their requests were usually granted. This was different from what Mr. Hayashi and Mr. Kaji explained. Mr. Takahara chose a job or a place on his personal declaration sheet. If he chose a place, for instance, saying, "I want to stay in the current department!," many such requests were taken into account, especially until the end of his thirties. When they reached their forties, that would be more difficult because posts would be more and more limited. That said, Mr. Takahara's *tenkin* to Hiroshima was not based on his request. While he had been in Tokyo for several years, he had never asked on his declaration sheet to send him back to his base, the Chūgoku area, nor to other cities. In order to keep living with his family, his wife and baby boy, he had requested to maintain his assignment in Tokyo.

The second irregularity was related to the reason for *tenkin*. One day, all of a sudden, he was called by his boss and asked if he was interested in going to an accounting school to update and enhance his knowledge on the subject and obtain a master's degree. It was one of the systems granted for government officials, which was called, "studying domestically." Mr. Takahara told me that the program was not only to acquire the latest accounting knowledge but also to fill vacancies at accounting schools. Due to governmental political commitment to increase the total number of accountants nationally, these accounting schools had been built in many universities in the early 2000s. However, most of the administrations of these schools had come up against a brick wall. Feeling responsible for the vacancies, the government had established the program, in which their officials could study. Generally, it was offered to only one worker per year among the three areas of Kinki, Chūgoku, and Shikoku a year. In the initial offer, Mr. Takahara had been told by his boss that the program would allow him to study while he would continuously receive the same salary as before. Mr. Takahara had thought it more interesting than competing for further promotion with other workers in the governmental office. Gradually, he had become more disciplined, regarding it as a good opportunity to learn finance, in which he had not majored during his years in college and little understood. He finally accepted the offer, taking his family together.

But third, in order to study, consequently, Mr. Takahara had to move alone to Osaka city from Hiroshima city by *tanshin funin*. As an area-based employee of Chūgoku region, he had once been required to move from his home in Tokyo to a post in the regional area, and then to apply for an accounting school from that post. Because the transfer was regularly conducted every July, and school started in April, he had worked in the position in Hiroshima for several months. Also, since there was no such accounting school in Hiroshima, he had to go to school in Osaka. The next April, he moved to Osaka, while he left his family in Hiroshima.

In these ways, male workers tended to accept *tenkin*, whether they preferred it or not, whether it truly developed their careers or not. This was how they sustained their jobs.

Women Going through First *Tenkin*

Such consciousness and attitudes were not peculiar to men. Female workers whom I interviewed also told me that, during the early stages of their career, they accepted *tenkin* as taken-for-granted.

There was one common practice of *tenkin* whereby newly entering employees are sent to local offices or factories as first assignments, as I described in chapter 1. Ms. Narita, a thirty-year-old career-track worker at a manufacturer had been transferred to a factory located in another prefecture right after she entered the firm. She had volunteered during her job-hunting interviews to be assigned to factories because she liked to watch things being made. During two years at the local factory, she learned about HR management, which led her to work in the HR department in the head office in her next career.

Ms. Harada, a thirty-four-year-old career-track worker at a petroleum company, was ordered to go to a refinery, right after entering the firm. When she heard about this assignment, she thought that it would be a good opportunity. The refinery to which she was sent was a major site of her company at the time, which changed later when the company was merged with another major manufacturer. Yet, it was very rare that a female employee was transferred there. In her company's history, she was the third person. She explained that by the time she entered the company and their president suddenly raised a new policy to hire more female career-track women, very few of them had been employed. She remembered, while she worked at the refinery, she had often heard that her boss had questioned why the department had the woman, meaning Ms. Harada, as a trainee. She also recalled the situation, saying, "It was not that I was not welcomed, but that I was rare." Still, for nearly two years, she enjoyed basic training for handling petroleum distribution. Then, one day, she was suddenly appointed to *tenkin* back to the head office in Tokyo to be in charge of recruitment of newly entering employees.

These initial trainings were also experienced by news writers, as Tachibana Newspaper Company explained to me above. Ms. Matsunaga, a thirty-two-year-old regular employee at Tachibana, originally from Chiba Prefecture, had been transferred to a Nara office for her initial training as a writer. She volunteered for this assignment because she wanted to go and live in a place where she had never been. She imagined it was warmer than in the Kantō area, which turned out to be wrong. She had barely thought of her next assignment, either. It was supposed to be a position inside the Osaka head office, as the managers of Tachibana Newspaper remarked. She had been completely "ignorant," she said, and also no one had told her about it. In Tachibana, this initial *tenkin* seemed to be shared as common sense, the same as other major newspaper companies.

Thus, these women who experienced their own *tenkin* during the early stages of their careers viewed it as part of their jobs. It was their problem, not of their employers if they had inconvenience in their private lives. In this sense, the experience of these women during the early stages of their careers was no different from the one for *salariiman*. In the structure where *salariiman* is reproducing cultural, gendered *tenkin*, *tenkin* is taken for granted.

QUESTIONS OF "CAREER"

The workers during the early stages of their careers in this chapter tended to embody the practice of *tenkin* in their life. They accepted their lives as they are. This was firstly because they were self-aware that they worked for the job that required *tenkin*. One of my informants, Ms. Hino, told me that *"tenkin* is a mind-set." With this mind, she raised her hand for overseas transfers and navigated her career. Such consciousness and attitudes were not rare among my informants. Another reason for the positive view was that they believed *tenkin* would develop their careers. Although mandatory *tenkin* could serve as a powerful tool to mess up workers' private lives, they tried to take advantage of it. These attitudes fit Ortner's concept of agency.

Behind this, there is a tendency, I argue, that students and young workers might be too mesmerized by the word, "career." Introduced to the Japanese business scene by American scholars on organizational culture and human resources,[4] the term, "career," has taken on a powerful meaning for Japanese workers over the last few decades, as if it were something that they can pursue independently and enthusiastically. But in Japan, where the Internal Labor Market holds sway, careers in the workplace could not always be pursued by the individuals but rather depended on their companies. If their company has a career-building system that involves *tenkin* requirements, the career path depends on *tenkin*, as the cases of the male employees in this chapter clarified. They had little chances of maneuvering their own careers. The students in the university and early-career workers seemed not to take in this fact, nor did many of my informants.

In fact, I occasionally encountered people during my fieldwork who strove to rid themselves of *tenkin* from the beginning. Such people tended to become specialists, including researchers, accountants, and administrators, which would allow them to be based in a certain laboratory or office, or career-track employees of firms only located in one area. The latter included career seekers in TV media, advertising firms, and foreign manufacturers, which had few branches to which to be transferred. Ten women out of twenty-three interviewees, who had experienced their husband's *tenkin* only, including Ms. Hayashi, the wife of Mr. Hayashi, were in this category. In addition, there were women who deliberately chose area-based jobs that did not require nationwide *tenkin*. For example, Ms. Takahara clearly stated that she had "no aspiration toward working hard [*baribari hataraku*]."[5] When she thought about her career, she wanted time to spend with their family at home and actually, she became a mother of three children.

Despite such deliberate avoidance of *tenkin*, however, since these women married men who had *tenkin*, they underwent various difficulties in their family lives. The next section moves on to workers' lives during their reproductive period.

NOTES

1. He meant the scene of a famous television drama, called *Mitokōmon*, in which a family crest is used as a symbol of irresistibility. *Mitokōmon* is a former feudal load of Mito Domain during the *Edo* period. In the drama, he travels all over Japan, aiming to make misgovernment in local cities better. Because he is a retired old man, he is not seen as a former lord. So, when he confronts a tyrant, he shows the family crest [*mondokoro*] printed on a seal case, so that the tyrant and other people have to prostrate themselves to him.

2. *Dosa mawari* means a practice that theatrical actors and actresses travel around countryside for their performance. *Dosa* is a derogatory term referring to a local city or countryside. By this word, Mr. Hayashi meant *tenkin* to local cities including those in Asia is dishonor.

3. Other than the Chūgoku area, there are eight areas: Hokkaido, Tōhoku, Kantō and Kōshin-etsu, Tōkai and Hokuriku, Kinki, Shikoku, Kyūshū, and Okinawa.

4. For example, one of them is Edgar H. Schein (1991).

5. *Baribari*, meaning "hard," derives from the onomatopoeic sound of crunching down on a rice cracker with one's teeth. The term *baribari hataraku* is used to describe, and even taunt, the increasing numbers of career women who work hard and for long hours, as if it were not a woman's role to do so. A synonym is *bari kyari*, or "hard career," which is increasingly employed these days to refer to a life of intense careerism. An antonym of this is *yuru kyari*, or "loose career." It practically means a life fairly seeking career and also enjoying private time. In other words, it denotes a way of living in which both work and private life are balanced. These terms were often used by my informants, instead of other words such as career track or work-life balance.

Chapter 4

Dual-Career Couples Living Apart

As the HR managers of the companies I interviewed explained in chapter 1, through *tenkin*, people tended to make choices in family formations: accompanying his/her spouse or moving alone to *tenkin* [*tanshin funin*]. Mr. Kaji and his wife chose the former, while Mr. Hayashi and Mr. Takahara and their wives experienced both. Both of the family practices rested on the gendered assumptions in which the male-breadwinner and female-homemaker model was seen as ideal and efficient not only at home but in society as a whole. For contemporary dual-career couples, too, these limited choices were only available and therefore incompatible with women's work lives, as a matter of course.

In order to retain their jobs, the first choice the women attempted to make was to send their spouses alone or move alone to *tenkin*. This was not only because they had no systems to allow them to move together, such as the spousal following leave system [*haigūsha dōkō kyūgyō seido*] which Motomachi Manufacturing recently started to provide, but also because their firms took the family separation due to *tenkin* for granted, as we saw chapter 1. Indeed, during my fieldwork, the word, *tanshin funin*, was more frequently heard from my interviewees, than the term, *tenkin*. This indicated, first, how common *tanshin funin* was among contemporary dual-career couples. Also, it manifested how uneasy they, mostly women, felt about the practice, in comparison to the practice of *tenkin* itself. This is because the dual-career couples were forced to live apart not only by *tenkin* itself but also by social assumptions based on the male-breadwinner and female-homemaker model. If they had a child, it was hardly possible to live a life without the support of their natal families. This research moreover laid bare another challenge for the dual-career living-apart couples, which was related to the reproductive roles. From their stories, it became clear that these "having-it-all" seekers do face a lot of struggles and therefore can be more vulnerable than they look.

GENDERED DECISIONS, NEW CHALLENGES

Associated with the male-breadwinner and female-homemaker model in Japan, men and women play different roles to complement each gender's incompetence and thereby to become full adults comprising a social whole (Edwards 1989). This division of labor contributes to organizing and maintaining the *ie* household.

The *ie* household system is the origin of the family structure in Japan. The system is a "corporate body, which owns household property, carries on a family business, and emphasizes the continuity of the family line and family business over generations" (Ochiai 1997). It also organizes power both within the household and among the households in the same lineage. It reifies hierarchies and defines duties and privileges by age and gender within the household and through traditional relationships with the other households based on a succession of main [*honke*] and branch [*bunke*] families (White 2002).

Members of the household are defined by a registration [*koseki*] system (Krogness 2011). The legal system was enacted by the *Meiji* government in 1898, initially to record Japanese population by household unit in the localities where they lived. It was then reformed after World War Two, in which a two-generational family became one unit. Under the system, members of the household are legally united on one sheet.

Inside a family as a group, people are given different roles, which are based on their genders and all aim to organize and maintain their *ie* household. Men are required to be breadwinners [*daikoku bashira*] and women are expected to be good wives and wise mothers [*ryōsai kenbo*] (Roberts 1994; North 2009). To accomplish these roles, men need women, or brides [*yome*], who manage domestic labor including care for all family members and women need men who provide economic security and proper representation for the family in the public domain.

When it comes to *tenkin*, to fulfill each role of the couple, if his (or her) spouse was not able to go along with the other for some reason, the worker went on *tenkin* alone by *tanshin funin*. Some of the women and men I interviewed did not use the term, *tanshin funin*, but "living-apart marriage" [*bekkyo-kon*], which the HR manager Ms. Meguro in chapter 1 also mentioned. This term had two meanings. First, it is an inclusive word, not necessarily connoting male domination in marriage. That is, the subject of living apart can be both partners in the couples, not one in the couple, often the husband, as *tanshin funin* implies. In fact, the couples who were willing to use the word "living apart" had cases that they both had the experience of *tenkin*. Second, from the expression of living-apart marriage, the couples I interviewed insinuated their sense of independence. For them, the ground of living apart may be in *tenkin*, but they had the sense that they chose the family formation. This stance was most obvious when my female interviewees told me stories about their relationships with their husband's relatives at home where he was born [*jikka*], in other words, their roles as *yome* [bride] in the *ie* household.

Staying Away from *Yome* Roles

A forty-six-year-old non-career-track regular employee at an airline company, Ms. Ōta, decided to live apart from her husband due to her *tenkin*. It had been five years since she left Kyūshū for Tokyo. Her *tenkin* was due to her company's business restructuring, by which the company ended its passenger handling at the airport there. Her *tenkin* was therefore similar to what had been seen in the 1950s' labor reorganization of blue-collar workers' employment in Japan, as I discussed in Introduction. Yet, Ms. Ōta took advantage of it. She manifested her freedom from her husband and his *ie*.

Her husband, who was five years older than Ms. Ōta, worked for another company in the airport, where the couple got to know each other. When Mr. Ōta heard about her decision of *tenkin* to Tokyo after several years of relationship, he urged her to decide whether she would marry him or end the relationship. She felt bad about ending the "inseparable relation [*kusare en*]" with him. In addition, she had low expectations of marriage. She told me, "I thought, maybe, I should marry at least once." Furthermore, her father was sick around the time, and also, he had just lost his father, Ms. Ōta's grandfather, and looked very depressed. She thought that her marriage would cheer up her father. She said, "I wanted my father to attend our wedding ceremony as an escort. It was filial piety." Then, she gave her boyfriend two conditions for marriage, that her husband should let her enjoy freedom, and that if the husband became fed up with her, he could end the marriage anytime. He agreed. Eventually, the couple married on the day Ms. Ōta received her *tenkin*. She was forty-one years old. She described her marriage as a contract. Actually, every year on their wedding anniversary, the couple confirmed if the contract had been fulfilled during the previous year. She clearly said, "Without *tenkin* I definitely would not have married him." She chose the option, as her pitiful boyfriend asked her to do so. Marriage was neither satisfaction nor fulfillment for her.

Her hesitation toward marriage originated from her negative image of the practice, which would deprive her of any freedom she used to enjoy while she was single. Her husband, as the only son in his family, was raised by his parents as the eldest son. This meant that he was cared for by his parents in all aspects. He had two sisters. The elder sister was married and lived in a neighbor prefecture. The younger sister divorced and lived near his house, visiting their sick mother twice a week. The divorce was perhaps, Ms. Ōta mentioned, because the sister had never become pregnant. Furthermore, Ms. Ōta's own childhood experience greatly influenced her. She grew up in a family in the Chūgoku area, where the *ie* household system was embodied in every part of people's lives. All in all, becoming an eldest son's bride [*yome*] was not a good option for her.

So, she took advantage of her *tanshin funin*. In response to my question, "What does *tenkin* mean to you?" Ms. Ōta answered that *tenkin* was "not bad" from her own point of view, although she expressed a feeling of pity for her mother-in-law who had difficulty hearing but played the mother's role to take care of her son, Ms. Ōta's husband. With the *tenkin* to Tokyo, she had been exempted from her role as the Ōta family's bride. In other words, her *tanshin funin* succeeded in detaching her from her husband and *ie* and gave her a better life. She planned to stay in the position in Tokyo for a few more years until she would be asked to take early retirement by her airline company.

Ms. Ōta's lives through *tenkin* and *tanshin funin* was pushed by her thoughts about the gendered family structure. She decided on her move to Tokyo, while evading gender roles that would be imposed on her by marriage. Such comparison and decision making influenced by the gendered roles were also experienced by other interviewees. For example, Ms. Fukushima, a forty-five years old dispatched worker, stated that she enjoyed her life apart from her husband's *ie* system not by her own *tenkin*, but by following the husband's *tenkin* every time. When I asked Ms. Fukushima until when she would keep moving with her husband, she replied that it would be "retirement." Then she started to mention her "fear" of going back into her husband's *ie*.

> We don't have a child, but I think that going back to Fukui Prefecture is taken for granted as the bride of the eldest son. It sounds conservative to you, and it really is. For me, if my husband says that he wishes to go back, I will follow. To be honest, I myself want to choose to go back to my parent's home in Toyama Prefecture, or we can also find our permanent home somewhere other than Fukui or Toyama, for example, in Tokyo or Sapporo where we enjoyed living for many years. I just want to live in a place where we can have fun.

While they embraced freedom on the one hand, they were always concerned about the very *ie* on the other hand. These cases indicated the continuing dominance of the gendered family structure in some contemporary *tenkin* couples' consciousness and actions. These women kept locating themselves in these very family structures.

Trying to Fulfill Reproductive Roles

Even if some women embraced living apart and subsequent freedom of their own, staying away from their domestic responsibility, if they were at younger ages, they had great struggles in balancing *tenkin* and pregnancy. Since they lived separately, either for their own *tenkin* or husbands' *tenkin*, and some of the husbands lived overseas, they had few or no chances for sexual activities to become pregnant during their reproductive period. These people's concerns and struggles were often more serious than those who made their lives by following their spouses' *tenkin*.

In the 1980s, when Yūko Tanaka's (1991) first study on *tanshin funin* was conducted, *tenkin* was experienced by managers who sought promotion. It came to involve non-managerial workers and blue-collar workers in the 1990s. At that time, the average age of the wives of men undergoing *tenkin* was 33.6 years old. This tendency helped direct social attention to the issues related to the practice of *tanshin funin*, such as high levels of stress and mental problems among corporate male workers as well as their family members who had to deal with their child's adolescence (Tanaka 2002). In contemporary *tenkin* practices, to the contrary, *tanshin funin* tended to overlap with Japanese family's reproductive ages. Those who had issues in reproductivity tended to show negative responses toward *tenkin*.

Yet, these attitudes were not only derived from their true desires for having children but also attributed to gender roles that married women were given in Japanese family structures. As previous studies have uncovered already (Lebra 1984; Edwards 1989; Rosenberger 2001, 2013; Aronsson 2012; Goldstein-Gidoni 2012; Roberts and Costantini 2023), women in Japan tend to see mothering as a natural role. In order to play the role, they marry and try to have a child soon after the marriage. Therefore, marriage often goes hand in hand with having children, even found in the latest study (Roberts 2016).

Indeed, many of my interviewees recalled that their successful number of children had been two, and until they reached the goal, they had been concerned about pregnancy. Some had been pressured by parents. For example, Ms. Harada, a thirty-four-year-old career-track worker in a manufacturer, had been explicitly told by her mother-in-law after she had given birth to her first child, "Only one child must make your son sad and lonely. And for you, childrearing experience begins at bearing a second child!" Although she underwent a miscarriage, she kept attempting to reach the number. She mentioned that during that time, she had put all her attention and energy into achieving the purpose, therefore, she could concentrate neither on her work nor her career.

In fact, for *tanshin-funin* couples who lived relatively close to each other, or at least within the country, the desire for a pregnancy was deeper and deeper. This contradiction was because, first, they noticed that *tanshin funin* might not be the only reason for non-pregnancy. These couples had chances to meet each other once or twice a month, more times than couples who lived far apart, between Japan and overseas, for example. However, after spending several months not achieving pregnancy, they began to wonder if they had some problems with their health, more specifically if they were infertile. This concern about possible infertility was often shared by couples in their later twenties and early thirties in particular. While going through the issue, they grew to see *tenkin* as an obstacle, although most of them did not see a gynecologist or urologist to find out what their problem was.

A thirty-four-year-old career-track worker at a local bank, Ms. Shimura, was worried about not being pregnant ever since she married and sent her husband on *tanshin funin* two years before. Ms. Shimura started working in 2003, right after she graduated from college. Ms. Shimura was attracted by the training that the bank would provide her with to become a banker. Her career-track employment category usually required the employees to have *tenkin* to different cities and regions. However, "by chance," she only had transfers four times between branches around the city of Hiroshima, where her bank's head office was located. She had actually witnessed only one case that one female career-track worker who had *tenkin* to a city on Shikoku Island. However, the worker ended up asking the HR managers of the bank to change her employment category to the area-based and also to transfer her back to the Chūgoku area, although the change caused a decrease in her pay.

Usually, such applications for category change were approved only twice a year, moreover, the reason for the change was taken into consideration. Generally, marriage had been the best reason for the approval, according to Ms. Shimura. People in her bank seemed to believe that married couples should live together and depriving them of their lives by *tenkin* was not legitimate. The above case had nothing to do with the worker's marriage. So, the worker's application for category change might be regarded as her selfish attitude, and therefore, she was sidelined, Ms. Shimura thought. In fact, the female worker had to stand by for approval from the HR department for several months in Shikoku, Ms. Shimura said. "It seemed to depend on whether the HR department could find a replacement for the post (in Shikoku)," she emphasized. In this episode, Ms. Shimura tried to explain to me how *tenkin* was mandatory but rare, if not zero, for female career-track workers. The bank attempted to put the consideration [*hairyo*] into practice not only for married female workers but for unmarried female workers as well.

Generally speaking, requests for *tenkin* were not granted, unless the worker applied through a "post challenge" system. It was a voluntary *tenkin* system, by which workers were able to know vacant posts open to them a few months before they submitted their transfer requests, and the HR department tried to match the posts with the applicants. In any case, the requirement and possibilities of *tenkin* increased when workers reached the managerial level. Ms. Shimura, who had climbed up the career ladder in the bank, was faced with the roadblock of its *tenkin* system at the time of our interview, anticipating that *tenkin* would continue to influence her marital life.

Her concern was also attributed to her husband's periodic *tenkin* and *tanshin funin*, which the couple had undergone for several years since before they got married. Her husband was a writer at a newspaper company. The couple met in Hiroshima, where the husband had been transferred as his first assignment as a news writer. Then he was soon transferred to Kumamoto Prefecture, and to Nagasaki Prefecture at two-year intervals, and then sent to Aichi Prefecture at the time of our interview. When he had the *tenkin* from Hiroshima to Kumamoto, Ms. Shimura had wanted to end the relationship and talked to him about it. But he did not want to separate and the couple decided to continue dating in a long-distance relationship. The living-apart relationship with a news writer was, yet, different from what other couples usually had by *tenkin*. Writers were usually not allowed to go out of their duty region even on their day off. Otherwise, they could not run to the crime scene or accident in a minute. If they had some reasons, such as personal errands that required them to leave the region, they had to report it to their boss, so that someone else could cover the absence. Because of this regulation, Ms. Shimura was always the one who visited him in Kumamoto Prefecture in their long-distance relationship, usually on weekends. For her, seeing him twice a month was not bad, in terms of their independent life. She could concentrate on her work on weekdays, while refreshing herself by weekend trips. For her, it was like a single life, dating her boyfriend only on weekends. She also mentioned that the distant relationship, or in her term, "letting him loose (literally, leaving him in the field)," was good for him to learn how to live by himself. Finally, the couple decided to marry while continuing the long-distance relationship.

Yet, when the husband was sent to Nagasaki Prefecture, Ms. Shimura once thought about quitting her job and moving to Nagasaki finally to live with her husband. However, she was sure that she would have difficulty finding a job there in which she would be able to take advantage of the skills that she had acquired in the past ten years. Her husband also agreed with this and said to her, "Even if you moved to Nagasaki, you would not be able to seek your career." She then chose to keep the status quo until the husband's next *tenkin*. Simultaneously she decided to acquire qualifications, such as the financial planner, that she expected to take more advantage of in case of changing her job in his next *tenkin*.

However, things surrounding her job grew complicated as the time went by. Around one year after her husband's *tenkin* to Nagasaki, Ms. Shimura was promoted in rank. It was not what she wished, but what her managers had decided. She had not hoped for further promotion because in her mind it would exhaust her with heavier duties and longer hours of work, and thereby, make it harder for her to go see her husband on weekends. She had even told her boss that she might eventually leave the bank to follow her husband's *tenkin*. But her managers pushed the promotion forward, despite Ms. Shimura's wish. It was, according to her, to enhance women's promotion as a whole and improve the bank's proportion of female managers. In other words, Ms. Shimura became the subject of her bank's advancement of female employees, initiated by the Abe government. She had no choice but to accept the offer. Yet, as she anticipated, she had to work harder [*seikin ga fueta*]. She had to stay in the office till late at night, ten or eleven p.m. to finish her job and meet the bank's numerical targets. Her employment type, which was changed to discretionary labor,[1] spurred her to make more efforts and achievements. Soon after that, Ms. Shimura broke her body [*karada wo kowashita*]. She had always thought that working too hard in a bank would not fit her, and she had been right.

Meanwhile, two months before our interview, her husband was transferred to Aichi Prefecture. This time, with her increasingly hectic working life, she decided to leave her job. It was after twelve years of service at the bank. At the same time, she found another job as an area-based career-track employee in a nationwide bank, which had offices in Aichi Prefecture. The job category is at the second rank of the course-based employment system, though we cannot simply compare which, between the career-track job in a local bank or the area-based career-track job in a nationwide bank, is higher in terms of rank, pay, and social reputation. She chose the new job for two reasons. First, she wanted to make the most of her previous career as a banker. Second, more importantly, with the employment type, the bank would transfer her to branches of other areas, which would allow her to continue her job while following her husband's next *tenkin*. This was usually called a spouse following *tenkin*, although Ms. Shimura seemed not to be aware of the name of the practice at her bank. From this time on, she decided to follow her husband, rather than sending him alone to *tenkin* by *tanshin funin*. She added, if her local bank had branches nationwide and allowed her to follow her husband while keeping her job, she might not have changed her job, but have tried to sort out her issues as the career-track banker. Or, if her husband's *tenkin* had been around the city of Hiroshima, she might not have abandoned her career. Both remained her hopes, though.

There was another factor that considerably impacted her decision making. It was having a child. For the past few years while the couple lived apart, Ms. Shimura did not conceive a child, despite her wish to have one. She had not used birth control, but she had not become pregnant. So she thought that her husband had worried whether it had been her problem. Her husband told her that they should have a pet but she knew that he wanted a child. So, she decided to live together and see if their luck would change.

Ms. Shimura had seen her friends and co-workers who also had struggled to become pregnant and then eventually left their jobs. The primary cause, she thought, had been the stress of achieving targets that they had been given by their bosses. Actually, some of them had infertility treatments. This made her think that she should have the treatment, too, although she had not done so at the time of our interview. She said that although her parents and parents-in-law were not pushy about having children, other workers in her workplace had often posed questions about it. Other people's reactions in the conversation made her feel that they blamed her for sending her husband alone to *tenkin*. Through these interactions, Ms. Shimura had become more and more worried about her husband's thoughts, whether he was bothered but had not told her the truth. She had lost the courage to go to see a gynecologist to make the issue clear. Instead, she chose the option to live together at her age of thirty-four.

To my question about the meaning of *tenkin*, she answered, "making a priority and causing a negative image." Every time she sent her husband alone to his *tenkin*, she "felt guilty." But she continued her career because she thought that having a job was part of her life, as almost all of my interviewees thought so, too. Also, she was encouraged by her husband to do so. Yet, with problems of non-pregnancy due to, as she believed, his *tanshin funin* and daily interactions at her workplace, she grew to feel vulnerable and opted out of pursuing a career, sweeping her genuine desire under the rug. At the time of her husband's *tenkin* to Aichi Prefecture, she changed her priority and made her mind up to quit, in order to bring an end to her ambivalent feelings.

Due to the tendency in the contemporary Japanese labor market that workers had *tenkin* in earlier stages of their career, fertility issues mattered more significantly to the living-apart couples of my study. It was not only from their personal wishes but also from the gendered assumptions on ideal Japanese family formation. Without much notice of the socialization, couples tended to face various kinds of concerns and distortions in their family practices through their living-apart marriage. My male informants were no exception. They needed to manage their careers for balancing *tenkin* and family practices.

Mr. Maruyama, who embraced an independent marital relationship with his wife caused by his *tenkin*, had to deal with infertility problems and negotiated a possible *tenkin* order. Mr. and Ms. Maruyama were both thirty-four years old. Mr. Maruyama worked for a manufacturer as a career-track engineer and Ms. Maruyama was a career-track worker at another manufacturer. I met the wife first, and the husband three months after that.

Mr. Maruyama had *tenkin* several times since he entered the company after earning a master's degree in civil engineering. He entered the petroleum company because he had thought it more interesting to manage a factory operation than to construct new buildings. Right after entering the company, Mr. Maruyama experienced his first *tenkin* to an oil refinery for training as a newly employed worker. Then he was assigned to one plant located in the Kantō area for several years, during which he met Ms. Maruyama. Subsequently, he was ordered sudden *tenkin* to the Tōhoku region to his great surprise. Several months after he moved by *tenkin*, the couple got married, but they continued to live apart. He was ambivalent about the decision. Mr. Maruyama wanted his girlfriend, Ms. Maruyama, to come to his place with him, but on the other hand, to do so, she would have to quit her job, which would be "wasteful" in Mr. Maruyama's term. He did not want her to give up her career. In total, the newlywed couple spent four years living apart, only talking over the internet phone every night and meeting twice a month at most.

Actually, during that time, Mr. Maruyama requested the HR department of his company to send him back to Tokyo earlier. His job had multiple phases during four years from the beginning to the completion of the construction. His skills as a civil engineer were mainly needed in the beginning and end, but hardly in the mid-term period. During that time, having few jobs to do, he truly wanted to return to Tokyo. Then he stipulated it on the online "self-declaration sheet," which allowed the workers in his company to declare whether he wanted transfer or not, just before an appraisal interview with their bosses usually held once a year in February. On the Intranet system, the company provided a box in which workers would tell about their "wish for transfer," with a pull-down menu including "I wish," "I don't wish," or "I don't have no special request so I will rely on the company's decision." When he was in Tōhoku, he chose "I wish" every year, with the reason, "I want to return to the head office," as he had been weary of his duties which had been decreasing day by day. Also, he had the reason to come back to Tokyo, to live with his wife. But his request was not accepted. The company wanted him to stay till the project was completed, maybe because there were few workers who could be in charge of that job in his company and who could replace him, although he did not ascertain the reason (with anyone). Mr. Maruyama succumbed to his firm's interests in personnel deployment.

As a result, the four years of the long-distance relationship in their early thirties caused a problem in the couple's birth plan. They had hoped for a child and met each other every two weekends at most while living apart, but Ms. Maruyama did not become pregnant.

Finally, after Mr. Maruyama returned to Tokyo, the couple went to a clinic and found an infertility problem. The couple soon started to undergo treatment, and at the time of our interviews, the issue was a major topic for both of them in relation to Mr. Maruyama's possibility of next *tenkin*, that time, overseas for an uncertain number of years. When a couple takes infertility treatment, they are required to make decisions on the types of treatment, and every month after the treatment, they just have to wait. This cycle needs a lot of energy and patience, with little assurance of success in getting pregnant. A sudden, mandatory *tenkin* overseas may bring all these efforts to naught.

So, Mr. Maruyama had tried to reject the possibility of the overseas *tenkin*. In the online self-declaration sheet, he chose the tab "I don't (wish for transfer)." But, to his great surprise, this action had caused trouble in his evaluation by his boss. He was told by his boss in his appraisal interview that selecting that tab would mean he could never be relied on by his company for faraway jobs.[2] Because he was a member of the company union, the company will never be able to order him to *tenkin*. If so, he might be regarded as useless by his company. Mr. Maruyama told me that it was like a light pressure. His "wish" for staying in the head office came not only from the challenge of the couple's pregnancy but also from the one for his career. He wanted to keep himself involved in his current head office job, as this was his first time to learn the management of the company as a whole, including the budget system. He also thought the "wish" was effective only for one year, until the next year's appraisal. From that experience, he realized that the company moved the employees who were available at any time, although he moaned it was unfair that someone like him would have to go (*tenkin*) again and again.

In the end, Mr. Maruyama chose the other button, "I don't have no special request so I rely on the company's decision." Then in the space to tell about family situations, he wrote, "My wife has to go to hospital." The space is usually provided for those who have special situations such as children and home that they want the HR department to take into account. He pinned his hope on the sentence about his "wife's hospital." By undergoing *tenkin* and the infertility issue, Mr. Maruyama had resisted the *tenkin* system of his company, but the only thing Mr. Maruyama could do was to wait and see the answer from his company by his next assignment.

Almost one year after the interview with Mr. Maruyama, his wife told me that the possibility of the husband's *tenkin* had disappeared due to his company's change of business strategy. Also, she had been expecting a baby after a series of infertility treatments. Going through struggles, resistance, and negotiations together at home as well as in the workplace, the couple won the lottery.

There was apparently one couple, Mr. and Ms. Sakura, whose wife mentioned her unwillingness for pregnancy. Ms. Sakura was a thirty-eight-year-old writer at a newspaper company and Mr. Sakura was one year older and worked for a construction company as a career-track engineer. Both of them held master's degrees, had entered their companies right after graduation, and had experienced *tenkin* several times, all inside Japan. As a news writer, she had had mandatory *tenkin* for her initial five years of training, in the same way as Tachibana Newspaper adopted and Ms. Matsunaga, the newspaper writer experienced. Mr. Sakura had been the subject of *tenkin* mainly in his training programs. At the time of our interviews, Ms. Sakura lived in Aichi Prefecture because of her *tenkin*. She had been sent to the position for promotion around one month before our interview. Mr. Sakura lived in Tokyo and spent weekdays in Yamanashi Prefecture working on a project.

The couple married eight years before our interview was held. At the time, they lived separately between Kantō and Kansai, due to Ms. Sakura's *tenkin*. Ms. Sakura mentioned two unique reasons that they had decided on the marriage. Around the time, while the couple had dated, Mr. Sakura's grandmother had passed away. Ms. Sakura wanted to go to the funeral, however, she thought it inappropriate that she would introduce herself to his relatives as a girlfriend. Another reason was related to her job. Because she handled news and accidents in her job, she imagined that, even if something happened to her, for example, if she was involved in a murder, he, as a boyfriend, would not be notified by her company. Yet, they discussed which surname they would choose for their marriage.[3] They decided on Mr. Sakura's surname because it was a little cooler than Ms. Sakura's, although she kept her maiden name at work. To me, too, she identified herself by her maiden name, as many of my interviewees did during my fieldwork. Mr. and Ms. Sakura married in their own ways, with few senses of roles and obligations usually embodied under the *ie* structure.

This unique relationship lasted until the time of our interview. Two years after their wedding, Ms. Sakura had *tenkin* back to Tokyo and the couple finally started to live together there in a house they bought together in the center of the city. For nearly seven years, Ms. Sakura accumulated her career based in Tokyo head quarters without *tenkin*. But after that period, she had a sudden *tenkin* to Aichi Prefecture by promotion to a chief position. It was right after the couple moved to a new house that they had built on land that Ms. Sakura had inherited from her grandfather. It was a three-household house with three different doors, located also in central Tokyo. The three households consisted of Mr. and Ms. Sakura, her natal parents, and her younger sister,[4] who was also a writer in another newspaper company, and the sister's husband. Leaving her husband in the house filled with her natal family members, Ms. Sakura re-started living apart.

After Ms. Sakura was transferred to the new position, the couple seldom saw each other, according to her. It was not simply because they lived apart, but rather because they had holidays on different schedules. Basically, as a news writer, Ms. Sakura was not allowed to leave a certain locale without notifying her boss, as in Ms. Shimura's husband's situation above. She had to be always ready to go running wherever and whenever some accidents occurred. So, if the couple wanted to meet each other, Mr. Sakura had to visit her from Yamanashi Prefecture. However, he only had Mondays off, which was a workday for Ms. Sakura.

Ms. Sakura remarked that she had seldom felt lonely, except at weekend dinners. She rarely thought about her husband during the day and tended to ignore text emails sent from her husband every night. She explained this attitude by describing herself as lazy. She often forgot that she was married. Besides, in response to my question about having a child, she answered that she had once discussed egg freezing with her husband but they had taken no actions so far. Ms. Sakura said:

> If I wanted to have a child . . . it is only for the future. I am only worried that I regretted some time that I had not given birth. I only have that kind of image of having a child. I am now thirty-eight years old and will be forty when this *tenkin* ends. We won't have time anyway, right?

The only tie between the couple seemed to be the fact that Mr. Sakura lived entrenched among Ms. Sakura's other family members.

Actually, her husband had an ambivalent feeling about his life in the house and his relationship with his wife, Ms. Sakura. When he had first heard the idea of the three-household living, he had thought it great. The major reason for this was that Mr. Sakura actually wished for a child. He then wished that his parents-in-law, Ms. Sakura's parents, would take full care of the child in the house. Also, he had presumed that Ms. Sakura's idea of cohabitation with her parents had originated from her implicit plan for having a child. But Ms. Sakura had left the house for her sudden *tenkin* at the age of thirty-eight, for two years. During our interview, Mr. Sakura repeatedly mentioned his wife's age and the period of *tenkin*. It was obvious that he was concerned about her biological clock for having a child. To him, her *tenkin* deprived him, or them from his viewpoint, of the plan for having a child. Before the *tenkin,* as Ms. Sakura also mentioned, the couple had discussed their plans to have a child, if not several times. They had never reached a conclusion, though.

The modification of his plan gradually made him feel difficulty in having a good relationship with his parents-in-law who lived downstairs. For example, he had felt uneasy about them, when he had received a phone call from the mother-in-law right after he had arrived at the home. He had felt that he was losing his freedom, although he had been aware that the parents were always worried about any trouble they might cause to him.

Having said that, he had never wished Ms. Sakura to quit her job. He said that her job as a writer was one of the reasons for marriage. He had enjoyed listening to her and talking with her, stimulated by her ways of thinking. He described his marriage as a relationship through which they can enhance each other's lives. On the contrary, if he saw his wife in the house as a homemaker, he would be depressed, he remarked. So, his wife's promotion itself was meaningful to him as well.

In addition, her *tenkin* brought him a challenge positively. Through her absence, he realized his love for her. He had felt lonely and needed his wife, although this brought about a negative challenge to him as well that he had to bear with her *tenkin*. This was why Mr. Sakura finally described her *tenkin* as a "challenge" to his life. All in all, yet, he tried to support her career in the same way as other couples.

These dual-career couples developed various resources to challenge the influence of *tenkin* and ensuing separation over their family lives. The resources included independent, supportive relationships and flexible minds and attitudes toward their lives, and communication skills that help to foster these relationships and views. With these resources, the couples went through the conventional *tenkin* practices and the separate livings caused by their *tenkin*.

Sustaining Dual Careers, Alone

If the living-apart couples had a child, their lives were also severely influenced by *tenkin*. The most common difficulty for these couples was child-caring became "one operation [*wan ope*]." Not surprisingly, the single operation was usually conducted by the wife, not the husband, although few of my informants gave reasonable explanations for why it was the case. While some mothers were physically needed by infants, most of the others tended to understand their family separation and mothers' burden under the gendered assumption that mothers are more responsible for childcare. Although the mothers themselves took the role for granted, they encountered various types of difficulties and therefore had to proceed with career management necessitated by the *tenkin* of their husbands and/or of themselves.

Ms. Hayashi, the wife of the *salariiman* in chapter 3 who worked for the railway company, clearly indicated the process of which the tide of her careers turned after she gave birth to her child. Introduced by her husband, I met Ms. Hayashi, a thirty-seven-year-old nurse in a private company in Kansai, in a café near her house, four months after the interview with the husband. By that time, already, Mr. Hayashi had ended his four-year *tenkin* in Hiroshima and been sent back to his company's head office in Osaka. The family was finally able to live together in their house, which they had bought right before Mr. Hayashi's *tenkin* to Hiroshima.

Ms. Hayashi used to be a hospital nurse, before she married her husband. Hearing about *tenkin* of her husband, her boyfriend at the time, to the Tokyo office, she instantly decided to quit her job and follow him. She did not even ask him about it. Mr. Hayashi recalled that Ms. Hayashi had truly wanted to go and live in Tokyo. He clearly remembered that she had told him that going to Tokyo would definitely be a once-in-a-lifetime experience for her. To obtain the chance, Ms. Hayashi had no hesitation or regret about quitting her job, she told me. Around the time, actually, she had been worried whether her work as a hospital nurse with night shifts had been suited to her, in other words, whether it would be her lifetime job. She recalled her thoughts at the time, "I was young. And maybe I wanted to change my life. My husband was astonished that I quit my job so suddenly, saying 'What?!'" The couple then got married and moved to Tokyo together.

During two years of *tenkin* in Tokyo, Ms. Hayashi experienced two non-regular jobs as a dispatched company nurse. She was content with the job, saying, "A hospital nurse has to cure sick patients. My role as a company nurse is to prevent disease and help employees keep good health. I think more deeply about the person. It is a one-to-one relationship." Also, under these jobs, she was able to learn more about using computers, which had increasingly occupied the medical workplace. All in all, her experience in Tokyo was beneficial to her. Of course, she enjoyed her life in Tokyo, as Mr. Hayashi described, "She worked in Marunouchi in her second job. She was very happy with it, enjoying going shopping. To maintain this life, we did not try to have a child."

When the couple came back to Osaka from Tokyo, Ms. Hayashi soon became pregnant. After giving birth to their first child, she soon began trying to return to work. She was hired by a manufacturer based in Osaka as a regularly employed company nurse. She recalled in the interview that she had been very thankful for the opportunity, for the fact that she had been employed even as a mother of one-year-old daughter. From the first day of her work, she had to shorten her working hours for two hours, one hour in the morning and one in the evening. In her team, only she took the shorter working-hour system. Faced with this fact, her feeling grew that she was "given great opportunities even though she was a regular worker having children."

Therefore, when her husband told her about the other *tenkin* order to Hiroshima, Ms. Hayashi had no intention of giving up her job. She did not want to lose her job. She told her husband that she would not go with him. She was determined to take care of her daughter alone in Osaka, while being pregnant with another baby.

This decision, however, had brought her ambivalence in the end. Although the couple had lived together in Hiroshima for almost two years while Ms. Hayashi had been on maternity and childcare leave, they lived apart for more than two years as a whole. During that time, Ms. Hayashi took care of their small children alone, as if she were a single mother. Because of this, almost all the rules at home were made by her, with no involvement of the father. She realized this when her husband returned and began living together again a few months before our interview. Sometimes her children were confused, she said. For example, Mr. Hayashi had a different rhythm. In the morning, she and her children were so busy preparing for leaving for work, school, and the daycare center, that they could not maintain the family rules, such as not watching TV during breakfast. Her husband was angry with it. Also, their conflicting schedules were problematic, too. Mr. Hayashi came home late when the children were sleeping and she was also very sleepy. All in all, she was often irritated at her husband's attitude and this made the children feel bad, she imagined. The relationship of the couple seemed to have changed due to the family separation when they had another child. She felt sorry about this change and thought her decision had been wrong. She said, "I should have followed him. I should not let him go *tanshin funin*."

She was thus regretful, also for an economic reason. While the couple lived together in Hiroshima during her childcare leave, they had to pay rent on two houses, one in Osaka and a condo in Hiroshima. Mr. Hayashi's company provided no financial support for housing such as the loans of houses provided by Okamoto Insurance, as depicted above. Also, Mr. Hayashi lost his *tanshin-funin* allowance once after the couple started to live together for her leave. This meant that while he was doing *tanshin funin* for his final two years after Ms. Hayashi ended her childcare leave, he was not eligible for the allowance anymore. Therefore, in her response to my question, "what does *tenkin* mean to you?" she said that "it was not a plus in every aspect."

Ms. Hayashi was a working mother and the primary caregiver of their children. Her husband's *tenkin* made her assume the role of single parent. Ms. Hayashi told me that she could not leave their children in her husband's care, because he had never tried it. She was sure that her husband would not want to do childcare and she had tried to ignore these attitudes of his in the home. It was she that had to adjust her life to his life, and therefore, she blamed herself for not following him in his *tenkin* to Hiroshima.

Nevertheless, she was able to maintain her job. It was because she was a specialist. The labor demand for nurses is higher than its supply in Japan (MHLW 2014). For nurses, generally, changing jobs was easier than for others, such as corporate workers. Despite that, maintaining her job while raising children created tension in the workplace, Ms. Hayashi inferred, because of her husband's *sarariiman*-based responses toward *tenkin*. Although she had tried her best, the outcome from her husband's *tenkin* made her vulnerable in her determination to continue her career. If she withdrew from her career, it would help to reproduce and reinforce her husband's *sarariiman* behavior at home.

Benefiting from Childcare Support

Many other informants received some help with childcare. The assistance included help from their own parents, parents-in-law, and public and private facilities, as previous studies described (Roberts 2011; Nosaka 2012).

Some couples lived with their parents. Mr. Sakura above had also anticipated this arrangement since before the couple had a child. A forty-year-old private school teacher and mother of thirteen-year-old son and ten-year-old daughter, Ms. Morii, also followed this pattern. Her husband, who had been together with her since they were students at university, was a career-track employee of a construction company and frequently had *tenkin* overseas. The first time was to England for one year, to study construction management. It happened around five years after their marriage, and when the husband left for England, Ms. Morii was pregnant with their second child. After the husband came back to Japan from the study, he became subject to *tenkin* to deal with his company's overseas business. He was assigned to positions in the Middle East, to handle a project of constructing big shopping malls there. After this *tenkin*, he came back to Japan briefly, but soon he was again transferred to Vietnam to manage another shopping mall project. Throughout these *tenkin* of her husband, Ms. Morii had never thought of quitting her responsible job as a private-school teacher, but only visited him in his transferred places. For example, during her second pregnancy, she flew to England during her summer vacation with their three-year-old son, which was an "awful experience; never again." She also visited him in Dubai with the two grown children during the school holidays. This was good for her to catch up with her friends who were also transferred there with their husbands during the same period.

Every time her husband had *tenkin*, she was determined to send him alone for two reasons. The first was their marital relationship. They were neither bonded to nor dependent on each other in their daily life. Ms. Morii had been busy teaching her private high-school students even on Saturdays. In addition, she had been a manager of academic counseling and was responsible for students' achievement in their school and career after graduation. Her husband, too, had seldom come home in the evening while he was in Japan. He also had to work on weekends to manage construction, in most cases, to catch up with delays arising due to bad weather. They barely had any time to spend with each other, except on Sunday evening for a few drinks together. These hectic lives of the couple had driven the husband to escape from his work life in Japan and challenge him to another world, England. Seeing her husband nearby and listening to his wish for *tenkin*, Ms. Morii decided to help him obtain the chance. On the day before her husband's interview for that voluntary *tenkin*, Ms. Morii had him rehearse with her until 3 a.m. While her husband was abroad, Ms. Morii kept encouraging him. She said:

I always say to my husband, "I will raise our children for you, so you do your best on your side." I know he was lonely, too, especially in Dubai, spending time alone doing nothing at home. He needed to call a driver to go out for anything, even for a tiny little thing. It must have been frustrating. But as a result, he could have changed his (work) life by the *tenkin*, right?

Ms. Morii could send the husband alone on *tenkin*, also because she was able to have sufficient assistance in childcare from her parents. When she ended her first childcare leave, she worried about how she would manage her childcare and work as a teacher. It was certain that she would not be able to come back home by the son's dinner time, let alone be on time for picking him up at a daycare center. Therefore, she decided to put him, and later her daughter as well, into a kindergarten and ask her parents, who lived in Saitama Prefecture at the time, to pick up and feed them at her house in Tokyo. Meanwhile, for the parents, the one-hour commute between two houses became harder and harder. Considering that Ms. Morii was the only child and she would eventually have to take care of her parents in the future, the couple decided to build a house that could accommodate the parents as well. She described the house as "not for two generations, but with more rooms," in which her parents could have their own space while taking full care of their grandchildren. The parents sold their house in Saitama Prefecture. The husband, originally from Hiroshima Prefecture, did not worry about his parents, who had already sold the house in Hiroshima and moved to Hyogo Prefecture. Furthermore the husband had been absent due to his frequent and sudden *tenkin*. So, he had no right to argue about the housing situation, as Ms. Morii explained,[5] "The cohabitation with my parents was decided willy-nilly. He understood that, otherwise, our home did not function properly." In addition to Ms. Morii's work, the husband's work and *tenkin* were used as a ground for cohabitation with the parents for practical reasons. Indeed, the couple did not attempt any legal changes in the family relationship and kept the husband's surname. Ms. Morii added that their children were happy living with their grandparents. Even if she asked the children whether they were interested in living with the father by following him to his *tenkin*, "they would certainly say 'no'. For them, our house is home."

This experience of a husband's *tanshin funin* for Ms. Morii overlapped with the cases of public teachers in Nagasaki (Connor 2010), in respect of their sense of duty in the marital relationship. First, the dual-income teachers in Connor's study had companion relationships in their marriage and family, based on their share of income and housework. In this course, they saw childrearing as a duty that they had to take as a member of the family, as a team (Connor 2010: 246). Although Ms. Morii considerably relied on her parents, she had a decent, responsible job and income. Rather than to "complementary incompetency" (Edwards 1989), the dual-career couple took pragmatic choices, not exactly on the assumption from the gender division of labor, but rather based on their own desires and necessities in family relationships.

In addition, Ms. Morii exerted another form of power in their marriage as her husband's best supporter. At the time of our interview, the husband was earning an MBA at a graduate school at his own expense, again encouraged by Ms. Morii. He enjoyed it and Ms. Morii overlapped her husband's challenge with her own. For her, his *tenkin* was his duty to make his life, as well as her life, richer. She guided the lives of her family, just as she did for her students at school as a teacher. Though these might be difficult without her job as a specialist or her parents living close, Ms. Morii's case also indicated that some dual-career couples embodied different marital relationships from the conventional patterns, seeing each other as a team member to live a better life together.

So, of course, if there were no relatives for childcare around, it made it difficult for mothers to keep balancing their own careers and childcare. A thirty-three-year-old writer at a news agency and mother of a three-year-old boy, Ms. Uchida, was able to build her childcare support during her husband's *tanshin funin*, but she struggled to imagine how to do so if she had had her own *tenkin*. Her husband, a prosecutor, had periodic *tenkin* every two to three years. The couple had got to know each other in Kyūshū, to which both of them had been transferred. It was Ms. Uchida's first assignment as a news writer. Two years later, she had her own periodic *tenkin* to Niigata Prefecture for the next two years. During that time, the couple got married, while the husband lived in Tokyo. It was the start of their long-distance marital life.

Ms. Uchida's next *tenkin* was to Sendai city. This made the couple happy because the distance to Tokyo became shorter. In the meantime, she experienced the Great Tohoku Earthquake. Her agency soon deployed as many writers as possible to various disaster sites. She was sent to Ishinomaki city where a great number of elementary school children lost their lives in the tsunami. She recalled her experience in the city as tough but fulfilling as a writer.

After this contingent assignment ended, she became pregnant, unexpectedly. Going through a little negotiation with her HR department, Ms. Uchida moved back to Tokyo when she started her maternity leave. At the time, her husband was there, too. He stayed with her during her childcare leave. Shortly thereafter, however, he had *tenkin* to Kyūshū again. This was the beginning of her struggles, which continued in her family life, as well as in her career, until the time of our interview.

Her first, most practical solution in the home was to hire a babysitter with a subsidy provided by her firm. In the beginning, actually, Ms. Uchida was a little negative about that solution. She was influenced by a common discourse that children ought to be raised by their parents, mothers in particular, in order to let the children develop their sense of love from the mothers (Lebra 1984). Ms. Uchida also held this view when she talked about work-life conflict in relation to childcare. But, in reality, her job as a news writer usually required irregular working hours including overnight shifts. Therefore, she had no way other than to take that option.

She paid 1,300 yen per hour for the babysitter who was introduced by the ward office. Meanwhile, the more Ms. Uchida asked the babysitter to spend with her son, the more she became satisfied with the service. She defined a "good" sitter as being flexible vis a vis her schedule and compatible with her son. With the job, she had to work overtime, work at home, or pick up her important phone at night at home. Her sitter answered her whenever she needed her. Furthermore, her son loved the sitter. He enjoyed talking, playing, and singing with her. Every time he spent evening with the sitter, at 9:30 in the evening, he wanted to go to bed straight away and soon got to sleep very satisfied. "Having her at home is better and more practical than calling my mother in Sapporo or my parents-in-law in Chiba for help, let alone my husband in Kyūshū. Oh, that is the most implausible choice, isn't it?" Ms. Uchida remarked.

Before she reached this stage of satisfaction at home, she had actually grappled with difficulties in her workplace as a "mama writer." Her boss, a chief of the department, was supportive, basically. For several months after she returned to her job post-childcare leave, she had been given a duty as a reserve corps writer, which had made her unsatisfied. She craved returning an independent writer. However, that required her to become a full-time unlimited writer, who could always stand by on the front line to deal with big news and political fraud. Her frustration with being put on a "mommy-track" at work was evident. If it had not been for her husband's *tenkin*, her situation at home could have been better, she thought. Then, she had a consultation with her boss, and told her everything. She was given one word by the female boss, "Why not?" It encouraged her. Subsequently, she started to work as the first mama writer in the news section of her company where she took charge of one ministry at a press club. She explained that she had no role models around her. Most of the female workers there, according to Ms. Uchida, had left the company due to work-life conflict, and some of them found new jobs, for example, in non-profit organizations. In her firm, female workers tended to withdraw from pursuing careers at childbirth, while male workers rarely did so, as seen in many other companies in Japan, she said. In the gendered workplace, she also had struggles in balancing her career and family life as the primary caregiver.

The next step forward for Ms. Uchida was to become an unlimited worker, as she used to be. By "unlimited," she meant night shifts, sudden phone calls, and readiness for the next *tenkin* particularly overseas. To manage the working hours and job requirements, she would have to find other ways to take care of her son, rather than only relying on the babysitter. If she did not request *tenkin* of the HR division, she would not be appointed for it for the next ten years. Moreover, she had not seen herself in the future as ever being interested in dealing with foreign affairs. It had been discomfiting for her to consider the possibility of *tanshin funin* and childcare overseas alone. Ms. Uchida heard of several heroic episodes in which single mothers in other firms brought their children to, for example, other Asian countries, Switzerland to study at international institutions, or even dangerous areas. But she concluded that they were very rare. "There is no end of looking up, while no end of looking down, either. To be honest, I understand there is a demand for full-time housewives," she said. This meant neither these heroic episodes nor other stories would help her survive her situation. In Japan it is rare that executives and professionals hire nannies, and in this study, too, Ms. Uchida was the only mother that put it into practice. She had to continue to find her own way by living through her own career.

Her boss had also told Ms. Uchida not to strain herself too much, because, she felt, the firm wanted her to become a role model of a mama writer in the long run. This meant to her that she did not have to work as hard as her male co-workers. It was a little frustrating to her, though. Hoping for her husband's return from *tanshin funin*, she continued to work. The time when she would be ready for challenging her career through her own *tenkin*, possibly by *tanshin funin*, was likely to come afterward.

"WORK-LIFE BALANCE" AND "WOMEN'S PROMOTION" AS FAÇADE

The above stories of the married women who decided to live apart from their families revealed that their careers are diverse, while they commonly had the taken-for-granted attitudes toward *tenkin*. One might recall my account of the university students and young workers in the previous chapter who seemed to think it would be easy to balance everything in their future work and family lives. The reality was different, however. The gap between the realities of *tenkin* and young workers' unconsciousness about it should be caused by the factor that the young workers have too many expectations about another shining concept, "work-life balance," believing that the government and corporations had made significant efforts. As Roberts (2005) puts it, however, work-life balance in Japan is only for the female workers to keep jobs, while raising children. Their promotions were barely considered. Or few male workers are included in this idea. In the society where using baby sitters or nannies was uncommon, the only viable option for the female career seekers was to live together with their parents and put family responsibilities onto the parents. This was no different for the dual-career couples who had to take the childcare responsibility during their one-operation periods due to *tenkin*. One of my informants, Ms. Honda, whose life I describe in the next chapter, noted that retaining careers during a childcare period without any support of his/her family must be tough "unless one is so courageous and vital."

Lives of "having-it-all" seekers in this chapter clarified women's career becomes vulnerable, if couples live apart due to *tenkin*. The dual-career couples' accounts in this study laid bare that the women are playing their care responsibility not because they naturally take it as their roles. It is rather because they are doing so by all means after a series of negotiations in their homes and workplaces. Since *tenkin*'s premise was on the male-breadwinner and female-homemaker model, little attention was paid to the struggles that these dual-career couples encounter due to their *tenkin*. The practice of consideration [*hairyo*] for women's *tenkin* while they have child- and family-care responsibilities merely helps them weaken their aspirations for careers, as Ms. Uchida's case indicated. It was merely a practice added to the surface of the gender-unequal employment structure. This is why they had to plan for many unexpected contingencies.

Moreover, because *tenkin* overlaps with dual-career workers' reproductive period, some living-apart couples who have difficulty in pregnancy become vulnerable, too. If not by inclination but for social pressure, most of the women I interviewed showed their willingness to have a child. In a society where the number of newly born children is ever decreasing, the fact that those who want to have a child cannot have a child due to *tenkin* could even be seen as a national matter. As my informants' narratives clearly show, *tenkin* is an obstacle to both gender equality and family formation.

NOTES

1. Discretionary labor, or *minashi rōdō*, is a law-based working style by which workers with certain jobs have discretion on how and when they work, according to the agreement with their employers.

2. The term, "a faraway job" [*tōku no shigoto*], seemed to designate two meanings. One was a distant job that would be assigned by *tenkin*. The other was a challenging job in respect of its contents, for example, to do a new job that required a new skill or specialty.

3. Japan's civil law, still called as Meiji 31 years Civil Code, which was put into force in 1898, stipulates that married couples have one surname of their *ie* household (Krogness 2011). Along with the registration [*koseki*] system, the conjugal system has generated a certain sense among the public that family are supposed to be one

team [*ittai*]. This logic is still used by the conservative government, despite a series of public movement.

4. Ms. Sakura had another younger brother and he would inherit their parents' house in Saitama Prefecture, where they had been brought up.

5. It is not normative for a man to live with his wife and her parents unless he is an adopted son in law. But the practice does occur nowadays, as a strategy to support dual worker couples, as Roberts (2011) discusses.

Chapter 5

Dual-Career Couples Collaborating

If workers and their spouses relied strictly on the male-breadwinner and female-homemaker model, their family formation through *tenkin* should be that wives follow [*tsuiteiku*] their husbands' *tenkin* with no reason. These people assumed the family style was natural and ideal, as the corporate managers in chapters 1 and 2 showed unless the wives had special reasons for not following their husbands, such as problems with their children's education.

The practice of following was reproduced by some of the dual-career couples I interviewed. Some women took it for granted. As a symbol of love, the term, "following," reinforced the aesthetic image of a trailing spouse who prioritizes her husband in the case of *tenkin*, as seen in Kurotani's (2005) research.

Yet, my informants were different in terms that they did not resign from their careers. All of the wives of dual-career couples sought to "have it all" and attempted to take advantage of *tenkin* even though they had a series of struggles and roadblocks in their lives when they followed their husbands' *tenkin*. The issues were caused by dual problems that occurred in both their workplaces and homes and were attributed to inflexibility based on the strong gendered assumptions. But the couples never gave up and enacted their agency, in cases of their overseas *tenkin* in particular. This final section elaborates on how these couples manage their dual careers.

NOVEL RESOURCES, NEW RELATIONSHIPS, BUT NEW ROADBLOCKS

For the contemporary dual-career couples, there were some corporate systems, which allowed the workers to follow their spouses' *tenkin*. One of them was the spouse following transfer system. This allows a worker to be transferred to the same place to which his/her spouse is transferred. Financial industries such as banks and general insurance companies tend to have the system, as they take *tenkin* for granted, as Okamoto Insurance claimed while trying to retain as many women workers as possible. Seven couples have used the system, which used to be called *Oshidori tenkin* ["lovebird transfer"] (Miyoshi 2009). Another system that contemporary Japanese companies have is to allow a worker to take leave while his/her spouse is transferred overseas. Two couples were expecting to use the system. The third system is the childcare leave system, provided by the Child- and Family-care Leave Law. Surprisingly thirteen couples, including eight cases of overseas *tenkin*, utilized the system. By re-inventing and grabbing these resources by themselves, these women attempted to pursue and enact their dual-career building, in the hopes that it would bring about better lives in both domestic and public spheres. But, the reality is this group also had their own struggles and issues as a result of their creative resourcefulness.

Tiding Over with Leave Systems

The childcare leave was the most utilized by my informants. Five cases were domestic *tenkin* and the duration of the leave was relatively shorter, from one to three years. The duration of eight overseas cases was longer, up to five years if women combined leaves of having two children.

If it was an overseas case, women enjoyed living in different countries, letting their own career take the back seat. In some cases, their husbands volunteered for *tenkin*. They raised their hand for the overseas *tenkin*, mostly for a short and limited period, that is, for three years at longest, as Ms. Morii's husband in chapter 4 experienced for his first overseas *tenkin*. These cases implied that some of *tenkin* were not necessarily ordered, although the workers were not fully aware, either, of the details of their *tenkin*, for example, what roles they would play and exactly when they were going to come back. Yet, many of the wives in these cases said that they had encouraged the husbands and pushed them to take the opportunities. Married to men who had jobs involving *tenkin*, these wives tried their best to enjoy their new lives overseas including their marital lives and childrearing.

Despite their enthusiastic embrace of their husband's *tenkin*, however, their lives after the leave did not always satisfy their original expectation. This was because, once they took advantage of *tenkin* as wives, they tended to be sidelined, regarded as workers not pushing their own careers. In this way, their careers backfired, casting a shadow on their own career even after the *tenkin* period ended, as Roberts (2020) also described.

A thirty-six-year-old career-track worker of a manufacturer and mother of a five-year-old daughter, Ms. Honda, was the one who had spent her whole childbirth and childcare leave of one and a half years overseas for her husband's *tenkin*. Her husband, who was two years older than Ms. Honda, used to work for the same manufacturer at the time of his *tenkin*. The couple, both researchers, had met in the company's main lab in the Kantō area and got married at around the age of thirty.

One year after their marriage, her husband volunteered to participate in a "global HR development system" with a recommendation by his boss in the lab. This system firstly provided the employee with a six-month English intensive training, aiming to send the employees later to foreign sites to work and study. Ms. Honda, as his wife, had also encouraged him to take the chance, envisaging that she would go and live overseas together. The husband was successfully selected and began the training.

When the husband's *tenkin* was almost decided, the couple made a plan. It was to have a child during his *tenkin*, so that the family would be able to live together in his transferred place, highly possibly in Malaysia. There, their company had the biggest production site overseas. As they desired, Ms. Honda became pregnant. They found it out around when her husband received the official announcement for the *tenkin* to Malaysia. Ms. Honda explained their situations at the time as follows:

> Our company used to have a strange rule that a transferee should fly alone to a post overseas, not accompanied by his family, for the time being, so that he can be settled in terms of the job as well as the life.[1] This rule has changed recently, but I always wondered how he could be settled without his family's support, right? Anyway, we decided that my husband would fly to Malaysia alone first, and then, I would follow when I begin my maternity leave (before giving birth to their child). At the time, I thought that I might feel easier with flying for several hours with my child in my belly, rather than with an infant onboard. Also, I was anxious about doing childcare alone. In addition, I thought that I should involve my husband in childrearing from the beginning so that he would become "*ikumen*."[2] I had heard from my co-workers who were mothers that it was important. Moreover, my pregnancy was going well and there seemed to be few risks in childbirth in Malaysia. Lastly, my mother promised me that she would fly there and help me. From all these mixed reasons, I made the decision. Eventually, I was able to stay and live in Malaysia with my husband as long as I could.

The family enjoyed the life in Malaysia. For Ms. Honda, it was an embodiment of experience as *tentsuma* or *chūtsuma*. The terms referred to a wife who had her husband's *tenkin* overseas or a wife who was settled overseas due to her husband's *tenkin* [*chūzai*],[3] respectively. Sometimes they are used in plural to reify a group or community of these wives, who took advantage of their husbands' *tenkin* overseas to feel privileged not only in living in foreign countries but also in becoming a member of the expat community.

In addition, *tentsuma* is a women's practice because there is no such word to describe a husband or husbands. Within the *tentsuma* community, Ms. Honda got to know and became friends with Japanese mothers who were also raising children. Her husband, moreover, was "pleased with living with his wife and daughter," said she with a smile. As she had expected, he had become "a child-caring father, although I do not want to give him hundred points." All of Ms. Honda's descriptions about her life in Malaysia resembled those of the wives in Kurotani's (2005) book. It seemed that she enjoyed her vacation overseas, even if it was relatively short.

Her time was up the next summer. Ms. Honda flew back to Tokyo to return to her work with a one-year-and-seven-month-old daughter. Her firm generally allowed its employees to take childcare leave until their children went into elementary school at six years old. Despite that, Ms. Honda decided to return at this timing for two related reasons. First, she considered her daughter's health condition in joining a daycare center. She had heard from other mothers that children tended to be infected with diseases for the initial few months at the center. If climates and temperatures between Malaysia and Japan had a big gap, her daughter would have more risks for diseases, she anticipated. She attempted to reduce the risk by flying back to Japan in the hot summer. Second, she had this concern in her mind, because she did not want to be disturbed while raising the daughter on her own. In fact, her husband wanted her to stay together until the next April. But, she wanted to return as early as she could, because she knew that getting accustomed to the work after the childbearing and child-caring break would be very hard, and "it was really so," she said.

For Ms. Honda, quitting was not an option, the same as many other women in this study. Actually during my fieldwork, I often heard that there were women who had made deliberate and inevitable decisions to quit their work after the childcare leave. Having faced gendered treatments in their workplaces, these women saw it impossible to balance their work and care of a newly born baby. Ms. Honda had different thoughts from her experience as *tentsuma*. She realized that she would not be able to behave like other *tentsuma* most of whom were full-time homemakers. They looked as if they devoted their whole lives to their husbands through housework and childcare, while they also enjoyed engaging with flower arrangement and interior decorating. She recognized that she had no such abilities, so going back to her work was the most rational choice.

Yet, before coming back, Ms. Honda actually had two troubles. One was to find a daycare center for her daughter. Generally, people are required to apply for a public daycare center that is located in the area of their residence. In other words, those who are not able to certify the residence are not eligible for the system. This was the case for Ms. Honda. While she was living in Malaysia with her husband, she was not a resident of Japan. This was caused by her firm's regulation that wives who followed their husbands also had to transfer their citizen registration to the transferred places to certify that the family lived together, perhaps for taxation, visa reasons, as well as their company's allowance. Therefore, Ms. Honda was stuck when she tried to apply for public daycare centers. Fortunately, however, there was one certified pre-school[4] near her parents' house in which she could squeeze her daughter, using her personal network. It was almost a miracle to find somewhere to put children into in the middle of a year, and it became nearly impossible after the enforcement of the "Comprehensive Support for Children and Child-rearing" (Cabinet Office 2016) that year, she added. At the time of her return, in 2011, the individual schools still had discretions in the enrollment.

Another trouble was about housing, which was related to the first trouble. She had to negotiate with her HR department about renting a company house. Before she flew to her husband's place in Malaysia, she lived in a company house where her husband had also lived together until his *tenkin*. She explained to me that her firm had a "cordial" system for company-owned housing, as "good, old Japanese company." When Ms. Honda reported her return to the HR department, she received a note that the company would prepare a company house for her and her daughter. Later, however, it turned out to be difficult. It was primarily due to the company's practice that an employee had "no right to choose" which house they live in, as Ms. Honda grumbled. It had been always the company that allocated their employees to vacant houses. Ms. Honda, however, had the technical problem with finding the daycare center for her daughter, as I described above. Meanwhile, one house was provided for her, but this restricted her choice of living places, so she declined it. The HR members did not like this and openly griped about her request, saying that they had never ever had such cases in the past. She understood that the company was reluctant to make an example of special treatment and thereby to handle similar requests from other employees, which might increase in the future along with further enhancement of women's working condition. She was disappointed but continued to negotiate with the company. At last, she was given the house in the desired location with a warning by the company, "You are allowed because you may have difficulty in childrearing without help of your parents who lived close." That is, the HR members emphasized that the facts that her daughter's daycare center was in the locale and that Ms. Honda had personally asked about the housing to them were not the reasons for the special treatment. Rather, the HR people wanted to show to other employees that they kindly considered Ms. Honda's child-caring situation as a mother. Eventually, for several months, she lived in the company house with her daughter, having support from her parents.

Troubles came to the couple one after the other. When her husband spent three years in Malaysia, he was suddenly assigned to a position in Osaka, to his astonishment and discouragement. According to Ms. Honda, her company had an "unspoken promise" that a transferee from an overseas post would return to a position in an area where he had worked before his transfer. To Ms. Honda's husband, the "area" meant Kantō. So, his assignment to a subsidiary in Osaka was a bolt out of the blue. Moreover, it was widely shared among workers in the company that *tenkin* to the position in Osaka would be long, sometimes with no end in the period. Also, the assignment given to him was too sudden. Usually, *tenkin* to Malaysia could last longer, up to five years. The husband was completely blind-sided. He then started to query his co-workers and previous bosses, "Why me?" and "Why this time?," craving reasonable answers for the *tenkin*. After the repeated round of hearings, he finally concluded that he was getting involved in the politics of the company, which made him increasingly suffer disappointment and resentment.

Notwithstanding, he took no action against the HR department because, as Ms. Honda explained, "he was a *sarariiman*." She then added:

> We have hardly ever heard of our employees receiving feedback from our HR department. The *(tenkin)* announcement was given on paper only. These days, it's been shared online, over the Intranet, though. Always no purposes, nor reasons are provided for us. Oh, actually, I once heard of a case that one Malaysian career-track employee who had graduated from university in Japan and entered our company received a sudden transfer order, and then approached one of our directors face to face and asked the reason for the assignment. This caused an uproar! Everyone was shocked and stunned at the fact that she verbally expressed the question. In our company, everyone is usually well-behaved.

In the end, Ms. Honda's husband accepted the order and flew to Osaka from Malaysia. Yet, simultaneously he started looking for another job. Ms. Honda noted that her husband had not been so eager to change jobs, but merely sought better working conditions. To put it otherwise, he had attempted to look for a job without *tenkin*. Also, his experience in Malaysia, through which he saw people changing their jobs frequently to seek better careers, gave legitimacy to his decision to leave the manufacturer. A few months after that, he found a job in a foreign firm and quit the manufacturer. This came as a surprise to the firm, as their retention rate was high. Since then, until the time of my interview with Ms. Honda, the husband was working for that foreign firm. Ms. Honda said, the firm had family-friendly policies in many aspects and one of them was flexible working hours. Thanks to the policy, he usually took their daughter to pre-school. Ms. Honda said that her husband had been satisfied with the change basically, except for the possibility of promotion. She explained that he had very little pay rise, in comparison to the manufacturer for which he used to work. "Once you became a member of the foreign companies' labor market, job hopping was the only way for pay increase," she said. After accepting the challenges and struggles of the *tenkin* practice, the husband turned his life for the better.

Actually, Ms. Honda, too, had a problem with her treatment at the manufacturer. When she returned from her childcare leave, she was assigned to a different job from what she had handled as a researcher. It was a planning job. Ms. Honda explained that it was due to reorganization that her company had handled right before her return. Just as her husband experienced, neither explanation nor feedback was provided to her by anyone. Since then for several years, she had wondered for how long and for what she would carry out the assignment, which was neither interesting nor building on her skills. Simultaneously, she had questioned why she could not have been promoted. Then, she had worried if her ability might have affected the treatment or whether her shorter working-hour arrangement had been problematic for her personnel evaluation. Yet, the latter was uncontrollable. She could not work a regular work schedule and still be on time to pick up her daughter at the daycare center, which was located at a one-hour-by-train distance from her workplace. All in all, she felt ambivalent about her current working conditions.

Ms. Honda herself, as a career-track employee, had the possibility of *tenkin*, but she believed that it would not happen in the future. She had never heard of women's *tenkin* in her company. In the first place, the company had hired few women in career-track positions. In her company, female workers seemed to be treated by gender. As Ms. Honda clarified, the company approved long years of childcare leave, up to the time when children become six years old. Men's *tanshin funin* was very common, according to Ms. Honda. The company seemed to take the male-breadwinner model for granted, as Hiroo Manufacturing in chapter 1 did. Ms. Honda added that, actually, her husband had been told by his co-workers, "You are indulging yourself by quitting only because you want to live with your family. Everyone strains oneself by *tanshin funin*!." She felt that this message had been directed to her as well, because she could not stand her husband's *tanshin funin* to Osaka, which would leave her to do childcare alone. However, Ms. Honda was cynical about these co-workers' attitudes, saying, "People in our company appreciated the good, old Japanese family." This norm of the company seemed to reproduce the gendered relationships of their employees. Yet, even Ms. Honda, who made sarcastic remarks about the company and other workers, believed that *tenkin* was not a practice that women should have to undertake.

This case of following indicated three salient points in terms of *tenkin* for married women. First, in Ms. Honda's company as well, men tended to be the main actors in *tenkin* and women were subjugated to being subordinates of their husbands. Her company had avoided sending women to *tenkin* to protect their gender, in the same way as it allowed female workers as mothers to take a long childcare leave to fulfill their motherhood. The company's practice of protection of women, contrary to their consideration of treatment, caused handicaps to women who worked very hard. To put it otherwise, in such a workplace, women were protected, not discriminated against, from the firm's point of view. In reality, though, they were not given chances to develop the resources that would be required to become managers.

Second, while this gendered structure seemed to be driven by the firm which forced the employees to meet the requirement of *tenkin*, it was adroitly reproduced by the employees themselves, even by the contemporary dual-career couples. Married women, such as Ms. Honda, embodied the gendered practice of following their spouses in every part of their private lives. However, the practice in itself was not compatible with the fact that these women had jobs and careers. This caused them struggles, although they were not clearly aware of the causes of the struggles and thereby ambivalent. Also, very few of the women I interviewed thought that they themselves could be the actors of *tenkin*. These states of their mind, to the contrary, allowed their employers to continuously perform their gendered practice surrounding *tenkin*.

Third, Ms. Honda's case further suggested that if couples worked for the same company, they were prone to reinforce the gendered norms in both workplaces and homes. While these couples were influenced by the same workplace norms, they shared the norms in their private realm as well. These norms were unlikely to be violated, since Japanese companies, or an "old, good Japanese company" in Ms. Honda's terms, tended to prefer retaining workers for their lifetimes to continually welcoming streams of newcomers, just as "old, good Japanese family" in her term again did. Consequently, as Alice Lam (1993) argued in relation to the tendency of the continuance of the Internal Labor Market, gender inequality was persistent in these companies. Although her husband could escape from the tradition, only because he was a man, and only after he had experienced *tenkin* overseas and learned the lives of people there, Ms. Honda continued to be stuck with gender-unequal workplace norms. Under the labor market, as a working mother with restrictions on working conditions, she had more difficulty in becoming a job-hopper. In the interview, Ms. Honda mentioned that the European company for which her husband worked provided a system that allowed its transferee to accompany his/her spouse who worked in the same company, as the company saw the family as a unit. This narrative meant that she and her husband envied that style. Since the couple lived in overseas and the husband changed his job to the one in the foreign firm, they had fostered such new desires. After all, her negotiation for making better lives continued.

Among forty female interviewees, two women were national government officials. One woman had her husband's *tenkin* only, and the other, Ms. Komine, had experienced both her own *tenkin* and her husband's *tenkin*. In the latter, she utilized the *tenkin*-related system that the government provided. In every point of her experience, she transformed the conventional practice of family through *tenkin*, according to her own thoughts, while striving to pursue her self-worth.

Ms. Komine was a thirty-seven-year-old career-track worker and mother of a six-year-old boy. She invited me to a government office in Kasumigaseki for an interview during her lunchtime. In a casual-looking meeting room, she frankly confessed her experiences of her own *tenkin*, husband's *tenkin*, childbearing, and family life. Her own *tenkin* took place five years after she entered the ministry. That *tenkin* was to Aichi Prefecture for two years, as was usual in her ministry. During the time, her boyfriend, whom she had known since college, also lived in Aichi Prefecture for his own *tenkin*. The boyfriend worked for a general insurance company. The couple married during their *tenkin* period. After two years of her assignment, she came back to Tokyo alone, leaving her husband in Aichi for another two years.

After that, the husband looked for a chance for overseas *tenkin*. According to Ms. Komine, the husband was considerably influenced by one of his bosses, with whom he had worked in Aichi Prefecture. The overseas *tenkin* of his company usually allowed the worker to learn the global insurance business. He preferred it to periodic nationwide transfers that were common in general insurance firms, as I kept describing throughout this study. However, the husband was not very good at English, compared to other workers who were fluent, so he had to find a post in a non-English-speaking country. The boss who had influenced him for the *tenkin* had been transferred to Brazil. So, he decided to volunteer for *tenkin* there and obtained it for his next assignment.

Ms. Komine was strategic, as many other women in this study were. Her husband told her about his aspiration for *tenkin* overseas. Around that time, she was turning thirty, and her biological clock was ticking. So she attempted to become pregnant and take childcare leave, aiming to follow him for his coming *tenkin*. The couple met each other almost every week. Then she achieved pregnancy.

Yet, as time went by, she became more and more anxious about raising her child in Brazil. She started to ask him, "Why Brazil? Why not other developed countries?" She had never been there so she was worried about everything. His answers to her questions were always "Don't worry." He listened to her in one ear and it went out the other ear, she recalled. He had seemed not to have any information, nor to try to obtain or find it out for her. Then he left first, going alone to Brazil. Ms. Komine gave birth to her son in Japan and four months after that she flew over to Brazil. Fortunately, she found that she had been overanxious. The couple enjoyed their life including childrearing in Brazil.

When nearly one year passed, however, one problem occurred. His *tenkin* there, which was to have ended in three years, was likely to be extended by another few years. Ms. Komine, on the other hand, was allowed to take her childcare leave for three years at longest. In order for the family to continue to live together, she would need another way. Then, the best strategy she could think of was to become pregnant with another child and extend her childcare leave for another few years.

> I had raised my first child in THAT completely new world so I had little time to worry about when his *tenkin* period would end. Then one day we found that maybe it would be long, longer than we had expected because everyone else (who were also transferred to the office from Japan) stayed longer. I thought, "it's gonna be bad. I would have to quit my job."
>
> My son was still very small and I thought taking him from his father was a bad idea. My husband also wanted to stay with his son.
>
> Then I thought, "if things go well, I can take the second childcare leave in a row." I had wanted to have another child anyway, for my son. My husband also agreed to the plan because he thought that having a brother was good from his own experience, too.

Things did not go as well as she expected, however. Ms. Komine tried to get pregnant for about one year, to no avail. She went to see a gynecologist. She had little hesitation about it because she saw Brazilian women often go there as if they went to see a counselor. Yet, no problem was found. Then she was prescribed a hormone drug and tried once, but her body showed an allergic reaction. She was also recommended to use an ova bank or a sperm bank, but she was not interested in further treatment. It was primarily because she had one child already. The second critical reason was that she became busy with study at graduate school.

At the time, Ms. Komine was desperate to find other ways to stay in Brazil, while keeping her job. She looked over the ministry Intranet, hoping to find the benefit the government offered to the officials, and also asked her co-workers to look for any provisions she would be able to use to extend her stay in Brazil. When she contacted the HR division of her ministry, she found one system of transfer [*shukkō*], or *tenkin*, that the ministry provided to a public firm located in the Japanese embassy in Brazil. However, she was not eligible for the *tenkin*. The ministry could not recommend to the position somebody who took leave and had no history of working experience right before the assignment, like her. Also, the HR division took her childrearing situation into consideration because, even if she obtained the post, it would restrict her work including working hours. So she gave up the idea.

The next plan that caught her attention was to use the "self-enlightenment leave system" by going to graduate school in Brazil. It allowed officials to take a two-year leave and go to school at their own expense if it could promote their skills to handle their jobs. She decided to apply for one university and passed the exam for a master's program in International Relations, and finally was able to extend her stay there for another two years. She recalled her experience as follows:

> Portuguese was the biggest problem. I had to write the application in Portuguese, discuss it in Portuguese, and write papers in Portuguese! Before then, I did not have enough time to study the language so I could only speak a little. I asked my Portuguese teacher and translator to revise my writing, a lot. I was crying every day for two months. Then at an entrance interview, the university greatly welcomed me, to my surprise. In Brazil, Japanese people are welcomed and respected all the time. It is because of the history of Japanese-Brazilians. Being Japanese outweighed my poor Portuguese skills! [laugh] After the entry, I had difficult times, mostly due to the language, but other students helped me, for example, waiting for me to finish my slow speech. My husband sometimes helped me with the language (since he had officially learned Portuguese at his firm's expense). He also took care of the child while I was studying. But, I always had resentment toward him, having brought me to the situation, saying, "If only you did not come to Brazil, I wouldn't have had such hard times." I thanked him in some ways, while I resented at him in other ways.

To my question about the reason why she could try so hard, she answered that she was only empowered by the fact that she did not want to lose her job. When she did her job hunting (in 2000), the market was at the peak of the employment ice age. So losing a job had scared her. If she were childless, she would have worked like a dog. Since she had the child, she had asked consideration of her situation from her employer. She wanted to keep her current position that allows her to balance her situation and the interesting work. "In the end, I have had a very challenging and risky life since my marriage. I confronted the several moments in which I would have to quit my job, but I got through them every time after all," she concluded. After a four-and-a-half-year leave in total, Ms. Komine returned to work in Japan, leaving her husband in Brazil. Eventually, the husband stayed for another year in Brazil, six years of *tenkin* period in total. The Komine family got through the period through Ms. Komine's adept strategizing, while maintaining their careers.

The couple might have another *tenkin* in both of their careers. Ms. Komine had suspended her requirement of *tenkin* on account of her son. Her co-workers, on the other hand, were sent to overseas positions. In her ministry, employees rarely had domestic *tenkin* in the middle of their career. She had a sense that she had narrowed her career by herself, but she had wanted to prioritize her son. She was aware at the time of the interview that her MA degree had not been taken advantage of in her career. In fact, her promotion in salary was two years behind due to the self-enlightenment leave. She had noticed the delay after she returned from the leave. Ms. Komine recalled that in Brazil she had had no time to think about such effects.

Her husband would also have possibilities of *tenkin* for his career. He might go to Brazil again or other few places where Portuguese was spoken. In case of his overseas *tenkin*, Ms. Komine would be able to use another leave system that would allow her to follow the husband's *tenkin* for three years, so she would follow him again by the time the son enters junior high school. After that, she thought that it would cause trouble if they change the son's educational environment often. Apparently, she had prioritized her spouse's career over hers, since she became a mother.

In fact, her attitudes as a working mother were significantly influenced by the workplace norms. Ms. Komine mentioned:

> I use a shorter-hour working system until this March, before my son starts to go to elementary school, although I usually cannot finish my job at four fifteen p.m. and work longer for another thirty minutes or an hour. But thanks to the *Abenomics*, I think I am provided favorable treatment. No one else in my division is using the shorter-hour working system, though.

Her working environment seemed to separate working mothers from those who were not. In other words, the national government also provided a mommy track in career-track employment. As a mother, she was subject to compromise her working style.

Ms. Komine went through a unique experience as a government official. She took advantage of the government's system to allow public officials to take time off to further their educations. However, she was given no chance to take advantage of the education she had received in her subsequent career. The employer, the government seemed not to be accustomed to promoting someone like her, she noted. They seemed to value employees who always prioritized career, including *tenkin*, over everything else, as also insinuated by Mr. Takahara in chapter 3, who therefore deliberately eschewed the career-track position. If career-track employees asked for dispensation from *tenkin*, they would stray off from the career-seeker course. This was what happened to women with children who usually had childcare responsibilities. On the contrary, few of these women were likely to complain about it. Their subjectivity was constructed to thank other employees for allowing them to prioritize family over career. In other words, the division of labor, often gendered, is remarkably taken for granted in Kasumigaseki.

Notwithstanding the workplace norms, Ms. Komine exerted agency. In her interactions with family, she developed new practices, such as an independent, supportive marital relationship, a flexible view on having a (second) child, and a communication skill that helps her to invoke these practices. In addition, Ms. Komine had a strong sense of self-worth and also enhanced it through her husband's *tenkin*. With these resources, she was able to navigate her life in her best way possible.

As such, while undergoing the practice of *tenkin*, women devised other practices to make their wishes come true in foreign countries where their husbands were transferred. The practices were sometimes provided by their employers through negotiation with their bosses or co-workers.

Negotiating with *Tenkin*-Related Systems

Ms. Ikeda, a forty-one-year-old career-track employee at a television station and mother of a six-year-old daughter and four-year-old son, clarified this point. Ms. Ikeda explained that she "followed" overseas *tenkin* of her husband, who worked for a manufacturer. She described the experience as "opening the door for a new life for her and her family."

Ms. Ikeda started to work right after graduating from university. Since then, she had devoted her energy to her job as a TV show director, traveling overseas often. She herself had no requirement of *tenkin*, because her TV station concentrated their operation in Tokyo and did not have such a practice. She gave up her holidays and her paid leave piled up and expired every year.[5] But she was ambitious for building her career instead. In her private life, she had a boyfriend, as well as many girl friends from university who were also single and who could get together with her for after-work drinks from midnight.

When she turned thirty-three years old, however, Ms. Ikeda began to question this life. First, in her work, she came to understand the limits of her skills by the age thirty. As a director of producing TV programs, she did not find herself a kind of genius. She was rather interested in people. This made her deliberate what kind of career she would pursue, whether she would continue to focus on people as a program producing director, or she would continue to climb up the career ladder as a career-track worker at the TV station.

Simultaneously, she started to think about her private life, wondering if she would never marry in her lifetime. Actually, senior women in her company tended to remain single or childless. Ms. Ikeda wondered what kind of jobs or careers she would be able to have if she married. Around that time, she rarely heard of social trends such as marriage-partner hunting [*konkatsu*], described by Dalton and Dales (2016), therefore, she was trying to look for her own answer by herself.

Then, Ms. Ikeda met her husband. One day, right before Christmas when she was unbelievably busy, one of her friends invited her to a drinking party, saying, "We are going to drink with men, and we reserved one seat for you. You must come." She soon found that she was only invited to balance the number of the participants and told the friend that she would probably not join. But in the end, from curiosity, she went to the party after work and met the man, who later became her husband.

Since the start of dating, Ms. Ikeda had been told by her boyfriend that he would have *tenkin* overseas within a few years. She thought it a great idea for him, and not bad for her, either. During the time, she had wanted time off from her work, to deliberate over her life in the thirties and afterward. Yet, she did not want to quit the company. Then, she decided to marry him, become pregnant, and move together with him to his *tenkin* in Canada during her childcare leave, utilizing the same tactics as my other informants who obtained the right to live overseas for their husbands' *tenkin*, as we saw in this chapter.

Ms. Ikeda was different from other women, though, and similar to Ms. Komine described earlier, in her strategy to stay with her husband in Canada as long as she could. She envisioned that this would allow her to enrich her private life while maintaining her career. To this end, she successfully conceived her second child and extended her childcare leave until the end of her husband's *tenkin*. This plan, surprisingly, was suggested by her boss:

> When I temporarily returned to Japan with my husband and daughter, for his job, I visited an HR manager to ask about the leave system. I expected my company had a leave system to follow a husband's *tenkin* overseas, as other companies had, you know. But I realized that such a system was not offered in our company. Then, I asked the manager directly, "Is there a way for me to extend my leave?" He then said, "If I tell you this, it may be harassment, but you may have THIS way only," pointing out the phrase, "childcare leave," written on a piece of paper in front of us. I had wanted two children, so I soon told him, "I understood." I didn't tell him specifically, like, "OK, I will make another one," though [laugh]. I understood that the HR manager would not complain to me if I used the childcare leave system and stayed in Canada.

Then soon thereafter, she became pregnant with her second child. She got to know a mama community in Canada who taught her about the midwife system, and she gave birth using the system. She described herself as "lucky."

Ms. Ikeda was the first childcare leaver having a second child in her company. After her case, a younger female employee also followed her husband's *tenkin* to the United States of America and lived there with the husband by taking childcare leaves consecutively. Ms. Ikeda talked about the case with a sense of a pride as a pioneer and as a precedent for her junior.

However, the *tenkin* experience of the family was not over. From April, three months after our interview, Ms. Ikeda's husband was going to be sent to Nepal for his next overseas *tenkin* assignment. In his company, transfers usually took place every three years. His three years in Japan were almost up.

This time, the couple had decided to send the husband to *tenkin* alone. It was a deliberate decision. In fact, the husband once attempted to decline the offer. It was for the children, especially for the second child, who would take an entrance exam for elementary school, as his sister, the couple's daughter, did. From their past experience, the couple learned that a father is indispensable to prepare for the exam, and he himself was willing to commit to it. When they had undergone their daughter's exam, the father, Mr. Ikeda, had cooked, played with the daughter, practiced gymnastics with her, and took her to their daycare center every day. He was a very involved father, Ms. Ikeda said, and she could not thank him enough. He also looked forward to the start of their daughter's new life in her elementary school from April. He worked for his family, Ms. Ikeda remarked.

On the other hand, for his career, he should take the chance. Around the time, his company reorganized its management and he would have more necessity to take posts overseas, if he wished to boost his career. After he received the offer of the *tenkin*, the couple had discussed it every night for about two months. They brainstormed pros and cons and came up with three decisive facts. One was that Ms. Ikeda must not quit her job. Both of them believed that Ms. Ikeda's life would be better with her job. In Ms. Ikeda's words during the interview, "I think only raising children at home warps people's views. Women by gender are earnest and capable for their jobs, so they should go outside and do what they can do. This helps this country develop more." Another was that in Nepal medical facilities for the children would not be well equipped. The last factor, their philosophy of childrearing, finally pushed his back. They wanted their children to go through various overseas experiences in the future. They had developed this view during their lives in Canada. "How come the father is not showing it by his attitude?" Ms. Ikeda asked him. He decided to go to Nepal alone. Ms. Ikeda had already asked her parents who lived in Saitama to help her out with childrearing while her husband was absent.

Yet, the couple had another plan. After the three years of *tenkin* to Nepal, the husband would be possibly sent to Singapore for his next post. Ms. Ikeda and their children planned to fly to the country and live there together when that happened. For this plan to come true, moreover, Ms. Ikeda would make the HR department of her company create a new system that would allow her to take a leave and follow her husband. It was the so-called following leave system. Ms. Ikeda insisted that using the system would be the best for balancing *tenkin* and family lives.

> The most necessary thing is to make a law about a leave system, I think. *Tenkin* and family lives conflict with each other because they are treated separately. If they were thought as a set, and moreover, if people considered them from a family's point of view, there would be a rationale for making the law. The matter should not be treated in each company separately (because it is about family). If there was any burden that law users had to take, they ought to. You know, even if we attempted something by ourselves, it would depend a great deal on our individual power, right? That includes what each of us individually has, such as our backbone, including our values, whether we have supportive parents, or whether we can afford to hire a babysitter. It really relies on what we have or not. This is unfair. So, making a law is the simple solution.

By this idea, she meant a law like the family-care and child-care leaves. However, it is hardly likely that the law would be legislated within three years, by the time she joined her husband's *tenkin* to Singapore. Therefore, she decided to take action in her company to make a new system. Around the time of our interview, she had tried to find the best way to stimulate and drive her company. "Our company likes to go along with other companies, so I will show our HR department examples of other TV stations which have already adopted such a system and also collect signatures from younger employees. I think setting up the system is meaningful to the younger workers. This is important to me as a pioneer and a leader of them," she mentioned.

Ms. Ikeda's strong volition for making the system was attributed to other three factors. First and foremost, she wanted to experience overseas life again. In response to my question, "What does *tenkin* mean to you?" she gave me two answers, "challenge" and "a door to a new world." Then she explained:

> I enjoyed the life (in Canada) very much. It was a great experience, too. I think turning a life every three years brings more fun to our life. I don't think living in one place forever is good. I don't get frustrated at all at entering a new community. I can make new friends. Also I want to do something that no one has experienced. In foreign countries, in particular, we can do what we cannot do in Japan, right? To us, our childrearing experience in Canada meant a lot as well. Our daughter went to a daycare center only for a year and half, and she learned to make her opinion and also listen to others. If I had no job, I would want my husband to move from one country to another (and she would move along with him, taking their children). I understand that it depends on the person, but some may prefer to be settled, others may already own a home. The other people may have sick parents. But it is THE family, I think. Once I decided to have family, I have combined my life with my family. Childrearing is one of my jobs. If

someone wants to have it all (including success in career, family, and children), I may describe him/her as selfish. It may sound like a Japanese thing to say, though.

Second, regarding her job, she was not very career oriented in her corporate hierarchical system. She thought that she would be bored at her job if she were promoted further, for example, to an executive. If someone wanted to be promoted for salary, it is understandable, but this was not her case. She had never been eager for fame. She had merely enjoyed her job. She said several times that she had been given too much salary. She might have mentioned it in comparison to her husband's job and salary in manufacturer. The family could live on the husband's salary only, she said. However, she did not want to, since she liked her job, even if she was not a career seeker. Actually, in my interview with Satomura Manufacturing, an HR staff, Ms. Yoda, mentioned that women tended to respect equality and justice, while men tended to prefer fame, title, power, responsibility, and salary by instinct, and this was why her company had fewer women in managerial positions. The narratives of Ms. Ikeda and Ms. Yoda suggested that their workplaces were both dominated by men who commonly sought fame, where female employees were marginalized.

Third, nevertheless, Ms. Ikeda always had craved for improvements in her life. One could see this in her relationship with her family. Initially, she had not been eager for her daughter to take the entrance exam for private elementary school. However, she changed her mind when she and her husband were told about their daughter by a teacher at a pre-school. The teacher told them that their daughter could not complete tasks that the teacher wanted her to do, because "You (the parents) always give assistance to your daughter in the end. You should rather help the daughter have responsibility for her own task until it is done. For this to happen, you must spend more time with the daughter and watch her develop a sense of responsibility. If you do so, the family would get through any troubles that might occur in the future." Ms. Ikeda recalled this as the moment that she was hit by a hammer. Until then, the family had enjoyed their life, but it had not empowered her daughter, she found. After that, she decided to spend more with the daughter, thinking about her.

Another experience, which was related to her childrearing and influenced her life as well, took place in her relationships with her bosses. When she returned from childcare leave in Canada, she had not been given any responsible job. It was firstly because she took a shorter-hour working style, similar to the other firms in this study according to the workers. In her company, when workers took the shorter-hour scheme, they could work for six hours. After their child became three years old, however, their salary decreased. Also, while they were taking the shorter-hour working system, they were given poorer evaluations than others. When this happened to her, her boss, who had always told her everything, wanted to discuss it with her. The boss told her that the HR department seemed to evaluate her lower, perhaps because of the shorter-hour working system. Then he suggested that, if possible, she finish taking it and re-start working for eight hours. She did. Meanwhile, her boss was replaced by a new boss. He suggested that she make a TV program that she would only be able to come up with. This meant that she could put her childcare experience into practice at her job. Finally Ms. Ikeda put an end to her temporary working style and came back to the front line as a TV program director. She recalled this experience as follows:

> Maybe when you are young, you have difficulty in compromising with the reality that you cannot work as you used to do when you were single. You have a huge dilemma. You have to care about what other people say. You may not have enough technique as a director. You may only have a small network. But I wasn't like that. I found out what I could only do in my department. In our TV station, making a top-rated program is everything (and she made it).

Influenced and empowered by other people, including her husband, children, bosses, and HR managers in the gendered workplace, she reflexively monitored her actions, formed her intentions, revised her relationships with others, and navigated her work and family life according to her desire.

The lives of women through *tenkin* suggested new practices of negotiation in their homes and workplaces. These workers negotiated with their spouses to understand each other and achieve their own desires for marriage, work, career, childrearing, and life on the whole. In so doing, they exerted their agencies empowered by various resources including their independent, supportive marital relationships, flexible views on their lives, and senses of self-worth. In their workplaces, the women also negotiated how they were able to manage their work and family lives. Through the practice, they tried to achieve their own desires in their careers as well as marital, childbearing, and child-caring lives.

In negotiation with managers and employers, some female workers shared their private situations, including birth plans, with managers. These attitudes used to result in making these workers sidelined from their careers. Some women in this study were different. By sharing privacy, they were able to pursue their desires for own careers and family lives.

A thirty-nine-year-old career-track employee and mother of two boys, Ms. Hino, achieved her desires in her career and family life by negotiation in her male-dominated workplace environment. Ms. Hino was introduced by Mr. Koyanagi at Motomachi Manufacturing after the first interview with them. Actually, I asked all the managers of the firms I visited on my initial round of fieldwork if they could introduce me to female workers who had experienced *tenkin*. Only two firms, Motomachi Manufacturing and Tachibana Newspaper accepted my request. I understood that the introductions were under the firms' control, but therefore, I also expected that they would be successful cases from the managers' point of view. Contrary to my anticipation, only Ms. Hino had a success story. Yet, my interview with her revealed that she also had a series of struggles behind the success.

Ms. Hino had a bachelor's degree in Chinese language, which affected her life substantially. During the recruiting process of Motomachi, she yearned for *tenkin* to China to make the most of her language proficiency. Ms. Hino was assigned to the firm's international sales department as she requested, although it required her to leave her hometown in Kansai. She was happy to accept it and live in Tokyo.

There, Ms. Hino found romantic love. She became engaged to her husband who also worked for Motomachi in the same office with her as a career-track employee, but was about to be transferred to a different city due to his *tenkin*. They decided the engagement at that time to maintain their relationship even while living apart from each other. Also, the 9/11 terror attacks to the World Trade Center that year was a catalyst for the decision. Ms. Hino said that they were scared at the reality of the buildings they had visited for their summer holiday a few months before instantly disappearing and they became obsessed with uncertain feelings for their future.[6] They thought that they should be together, even if it did not include cohabitation, as other women in my study also sought and put it into practice.

Soon after, however, Ms. Hino became sick and had to take leave for eight months. The disease was tuberculosis. The couple found out about it while they were on a honeymoon. Ms. Hino was tormented with a deep shock and miserable feeling. She even thought of leaving her job, and in fact she applied for graduate school, seeking another career, though she did not pass the second admissions interview.

After her recovery, Ms. Hino started again to look for chances for *tenkin* to China, but her desire did not soon materialize. Her assignment was changed to a secondary job in the same sales department by her boss under the guise of consideration for her health. When one *tenkin* offer to China came before her, one male manager at the HR department, baffled by her wish, said, "You are married. So you will not accept (it, will you)?!" Faced with such discrimination, she lost her courage and did not push her desire any further.

But Ms. Hino did not lose her fighting spirit. Rather, she resisted it. Three forces influenced her that time. First, she "exploded in herself." After the discrimination, Ms. Hino had kept quiet for a while. But soon, she felt so frustrated with other people being too nice to her. Since childhood, she had not been a person who wanted to be cared for by someone. Rather, on many occasions, for example, when she studied abroad in a college in China for one year and when she had tuberculosis, she always took care of her. So, while craving to work more, she exploded in irritation. Second, her mother pushed Ms. Hino to try harder. When Ms. Hino shared her dilemma with the mother, she was told, "You made the situation yourself. So YOU must get over this!" Ms. Hino was empowered. The last force was related to her birth plan. After the disease, she had been told by her medical doctor that she must not be pregnant for the following three years, as giving birth would kill her. This became a good reason for her to concentrate on work for the period. Given these forces, Ms. Hino was tenacious in producing more output than others for about half a year and awaited the next opportunity.

Finally, a chance appeared. Ms. Hino heard a rumor that her firm was thinking of transferring her to China as the first female employee transferred overseas. She went to see her boss straightaway and insisted, "I have to go now!" Though her boss was still concerned about her health and husband, she kept asserting that everything was fine. At last, Ms. Hino obtained the opportunity and flew to China, leaving her husband in Japan. During her two-and-a-half-year *tenkin*, she devoted all her energy to her sales job, striving to keep up with the high speed of Chinese business. She was so busy that she needed a maid at home, who helped her with household chores, including seasonal changes of her clothes.

When Ms. Hino's *tenkin* period was almost over, four years had passed since she had married. She was in her late twenties. Then she invoked the following unique strategy to make her birth plan come true:

> To my (male) boss in China, I revealed my wish for pregnancy, saying, "I am almost thirty, so I want to think (about having a child)." Otherwise, I might have been made to stay there much longer.
>
> Then soon after (coming back to Japan), I became pregnant! It surprised everyone! My next boss in Japan told me, "I did not know!" (that Ms. Hino is going to take a childcare leave) [laugh] But, he added, "All right then. Come back to the (same) position after your leave."

She negotiated with her boss about her return from China and birth plan. Moreover, she convinced another boss of her career after the leave.

Her practice of negotiation continued. A few years after the childbirth, she wanted to have another child. She said to me that she had needed to make a sibling for her "too naughty" son. That time again, Ms. Hino talked with the boss about her pregnancy:

> I asked my boss, "I want to have a second child, so can I?" Even before I asked, the boss had also asked me about it. He was such a person. So I asked him like that. Then he said, "Can you wait for another half year?" (during which the firm

wanted her to take a promotion exam).[7] I asked him again assertively, more than the first time, "I will do my best for that period, so can I?" He said, "Yes!" Actually I wanted to have two children with a three-year difference in their ages, but because of this, it became four.

We had such conversations in my feedback interviews for my sales records and career objectives, conducted every half a year. I did not feel uncomfortable with him. I thought he was kind as he considered my career including my life planning. Other (female) workers had one child, but not two. Some were unmarried. I was anxious about raising two children as there were few role models around me. To have the second child, there was a ceiling for childrearing of two children, but more than that, for taking the leave twice.

After her second son was born, Ms. Hino again returned to the same position in the global HR management, in which she could continue to take advantage of her experience of *tenkin* to China. She was content with the position at the time of our interview. In response to my question about the meaning of *tenkin,* she emphasized two words, a "career ladder" and "mindset." After all constraints, struggles, and challenges in her negotiation over *tenkin* and birth plans, Ms. Hino constructed her subjectivity as a career-track worker of Motomachi Manufacturing. Yet, she did so in her own way as a career seeker as well as a mother.

Ms. Hino's career was aided by her negotiation at home, the same as other working mothers in my study. She had frequent conversation with her husband about her ambition for next *tenkin*, and she had already planned to take her sons together and let her husband follow them in that case. Her "husband is unique and not much career-oriented," she said. From this narrative, with the term, *otto*, one may infer Ms. Hino's independent marital relationship with her husband, as indicated by some other couples in this study. Ms. Hino was sure that he understood her desire for career and did not mind prioritizing it. She attributed this to her husband's childhood experience of his mother, a graduate of the University of Tokyo, living away from him for her job. Also in fact, Ms. Hino received more salary with a higher rank than her husband, who was three years older. The couple was even ready to sell their house whenever necessary for her career. It had already been in their script since they bought it in a good location near their workplace. The couple had a negotiable relationship at home, as they did at the workplace. This empowered Ms. Hino as a working mother at Motomachi.

Later, her wish for another *tenkin* was realized. In January 2017, in response to my new year greetings, Ms. Hino sent me a short email, saying that she would leave to China for *tenkin* the very next day. Her husband had already decided to take the three-year spousal following leave, which had been newly adopted as a system in Motomachi, as part of the "diversity and inclusion" reform. The system became available only several months before the couple used it. The husband then would follow her with their two sons from April. Ms. Hino's husband would be the second taker of the leave among all the employees and the first taker as a man. The vice president, Mr. Tsuchida told me that the firm had had no intention of offering another job in China for Ms. Hino's husband, and on the contrary, he had asked the husband in private if it had been a deliberate decision. However, the husband had responded, "Our experience overseas would contribute to our sons' futures and I would take care of them there." This implied that the manager was concerned about the delay in the husband's career, and the husband was also aware of it. In fact, many of my informants who had used such a leave system due to *tenkin*, ended up in delaying their own careers, as in Ms. Aoi's case below. Ms. Hino noted in her email to me that she was grateful for all the understanding and support from her parents, in-laws, as well as her husband and children, and made up her mind to challenge the new stage. By this challenge, *tenkin* in Motomachi changed to a gender-equal practice, as I discussed it in chapter 2.

Ms. Hino was constrained and empowered in striving to accomplish her career and family life through *tenkin*. In her work, she struggled against her disease and discrimination against the disease and her gender. The disease caused difficulties in her marital life, as well. But she never gave up.

Various resources that she had cultivated through her life enabled her to get over the constraints. First, at home, her independent, supportive relationship with her husband, flexible views on her life, and senses of self-worth were key resources in her pursuit and enactment of her career. In addition, her good communication skill played a pivotal part not only to invoke these resources in her family, including her relationships with her natal mother and mother-in-law. The very skill enabled her to bring her desires to her workplace and go negotiate with her employers. This made her different from the workers who could develop few resources to overcome nonnegotiable workplace and family structures. That is to say, the communication skill played the central role among the other resources in her achievement. As the result of these interactions with her bosses with regard to *tenkin*, she constructed her subjectivity as a career-track employee beyond the dominant gendered norms.

In so doing, Ms. Hino was also empowered by her company, Motomachi Manufacturing. Although the managers and employees displayed a number of gender-blind attitudes, as I described in chapter 1 and 2, Motomachi had its own purpose, to succeed in the global business, for sending Ms. Hino to China. The employer provided opportunities of daily conversation and feedback in the workplace. The purpose, practice, and norm drove the firm to go negotiate and make a less-gender-minded relationship with her. To put it another way, her achievement in her career also depended on her firm's utilization of her as a career-track employee in its pursuit and enactment of the efficiency. To this end, indeed, Motomachi sidelined Ms. Hino's husband on its assumption of the division of labor, and this revealed that the company was yet unable to make the most use of both employees of its dual-career couples. Notwithstanding, the company invoked change of its gendered practice of *tenkin*, so that Ms. Hino could achieve her career and family lives. This case in its entirety indicates that, where there is a practice of negotiation, there is a chance, at least a little, for change in the gendered structure. The whole process exemplifies Ortner's (2006) concept of agency.

Yet, there remained one fundamental issues for *tenkin* for dual-career couples: whether the couple in their prime reproductive periods could pursue both of their careers through *tenkin*? Even though these workers were provided with opportunities for negotiation by their employees, even if these workers' desires for careers were satisfied, as Ms. Hino above showed, the dual-career couples in this study, thirteen women and one man who experienced both their own and spouses' *tenkin*, struggled to pursue both of their careers through *tenkin*.

Among the workers, however, some strategically and intentionally negotiated their requirement of *tenkin* itself, but thereby strove to build their careers, both of the husbands and wives. In this final section, I spotlight these people's careers in forging the practices of *tenkin*, which were also new phenomena in Japanese workplaces.

Ms. Aoi, a thirty-five-year-old career-track employee at a trading firm and mother of three children, aged one, three, and five, entered the company right after she graduated from university. There she had majored in history of science and this inter-disciplinary specialty led her to choose a job in the trading company. Among about forty co-workers who entered the firm in the same year, there were three female workers. All of them had continued their jobs, after their marriage and childbearing.

Ms. Aoi had her own *tenkin*. Five years after she had entered the company, she was transferred to New York as a trainee for one and half years. She had not wished for this assignment. Around that time, her mother, who lived in her hometown in Kyūshū island, fell ill and she was worried about her treatment. Her boss at the time knew of it and was also concerned about her mother's health. He gave her time to deliberate about *tenkin*. She finally made the decision to accept the offer for several reasons. First, the duration of *tenkin* was fixed and short. Also, she was relieved that her father said he would support his wife. In addition, she was aware that such an opportunity would never come again. After all there was no good reason left in front of her to reject the *tenkin*. She enjoyed her work as a trainee. Also, living in the city influenced her in her later decision-making.

A year after she came back from New York, she married a man who also worked for the same trading firm. Soon after that, her husband received a *tenkin* order to New York. Ms. Aoi was pregnant with her first child at the time. Also, her firm was decreasing her investment work for some reason, making her feel bored at her job. Therefore, Ms. Aoi decided to follow her husband, taking the following leave that her firm unofficially provided its employees at the time. She flew to the United States six months after her husband did. Upon arriving in New York, Ms. Aoi looked for a hospital and gave birth to her daughter. In our interview, she recalled her childrearing there as her good time.

But the happy life did not last so long. After almost one and a half years, her husband suddenly received another *tenkin* to Dallas, which was the start of Ms. Aoi's challenges and struggles with her husband's *tenkin*. In the beginning, she thought that her journey would end in New York. Going to Dallas was a bolt from the blue. She had no friends there. But for her daughter, who was attached to her father, Ms. Aoi decided to move with her husband. Then she start negotiating with her company if she could work there. She actually had an offer from the local branch where her husband worked, and he asked the head office in Japan if that would be possible. But it turned out to be difficult. Then she decided to have a second child to extend her leave and stay in Dallas with her husband as long as possible.

Her husband's boss at the Tokyo head office explained that her request to work in Dallas had been denied because the position she had been offered was for a local employee rather than a transferee from Japan. But Ms. Aoi later heard another story from a different source. The real reason was that the HR department did not want to make "unfair" treatment of co-worker couples on *tenkin*. Around that time, another couple had been transferred together to the same place, which had caused other employees to complain loudly about fair treatment in the use of *tenkin*. Also, "fairness" seemed to assume the "sameness" among all the workers involved. Negotiation was not welcomed in her company.

Ms. Aoi decided to follow her husband to Dallas with her baby daughter, switching the leave from following leave to childcare leave. In the meantime, she successfully became pregnant and in the next year, she switched her childcare leaves from her daughter to the second child. This ended up as three-and-a-half years of consecutive leave for her in the United States.

By the time her husband heard rumors of his possible *tenkin* back to Tokyo, Ms. Aoi was desperate to return to her job. So, the couple unofficially negotiated with the HR department, to find a successor for her husband in Dallas, so that they could come back to Japan together.

It was after that Ms. Aoi realized the obstacles she faced in pursuing her own career. First, her promotion had been delayed and her salary was less than that of her colleagues because her rank had not gone up during her absence, in the same ways as other interviewees in this study experienced.

Her co-workers who had entered the company in the same year with her were already in section-chief positions. Meanwhile, Ms. Aoi became unexpectedly pregnant with her third child. During this time, her boss asked her whether she could take her own *tenkin* overseas for the next step in her career. This was how the trading company usually promoted employees. She said:

> The boss (at the time) was eager to know what I think of my career. He tried to persuade me to say that I am willing to do *tenkin*. I parried it, saying, "I cannot commit myself to it. We have many significant jobs here (in Tokyo) so why should I?" Actually, in terms of the contents of the job that I have been handling, I think they are more interesting and also worthwhile jobs in Tokyo. I can control all the operations overseas.
>
> I just cannot imagine what it would be like in a foreign country with my three children, even if my husband came with me. In the U.S., for example, I think parents have to go to children's school quite often. So, living in foreign countries is advantageous to children, generally speaking, but not to parents who will be transferred like me. I know that this would be disadvantageous to my career, though.

With her baby still small, she had little intention of accepting *tenkin* overseas. Thus she tried not to give a decisive answer and kept telling her boss that there were many important divisions of the firm in Tokyo where she could find her next position. Although her firm seemed to expect her to take *tenkin* for her career and its business, it did not provide her with any solution for her childrearing overseas. The result was that Ms. Aoi as a career-seeking mother became a vulnerable subject who managed to maintain her job only, as she put it, "by the skin of their teeth."

Ms. Aoi's husband also had a possibility of *tenkin* in his job. The husband as well had asked consideration from the HR division to assign him to domestic posts. Since the husband had been in the United States for six years, usually he was not supposed to be sent anywhere overseas. But *tenkin* orders could occur anytime, according to the company's business needs. Ms. Aoi said that her husband had unofficially negotiated with his boss who had the right to decide the husband's transfer. In fact, Ms. Aoi would be eligible for another following leave. When she firstly took leave to follow her husband to New York, it was not a system yet. Later, her company established it as a system and set a regulation in which employees can take it only one time for three years in their lifetime. But if she used the system, her career would face a dead-end, she anticipated.

Ms. Aoi as the career-track employee at the trading firm exerted agency in both her career and family. Her independent, supportive marital relationship, flexible attitudes toward her life, sense of self-worth, as well as communication skills as resources helped her go negotiate over *tenkin*, itself, and family lives. Her bosses also acknowledged her abilities and tried to boost her career through *tenkin*. The attempt, however, turned out to be a trouble.

This inconsistency was caused by the fact that the firm seemed to have no idea of how to treat two employees equally as a couple when it came to the practice of *tenkin*. Many other firms in this study also struggled with this and ended up treating one of them, female workers in most cases, as the second players. This was because, to repeat, their practices of *tenkin* overlapped with workers' reproductive periods, and also fundamentally rested on the division of labor, if not necessarily gendered, as Ms. Hino family above already showed. Now that an increasing number of couples are both career-seekers, presumably in the same company, such troubles should not be overlooked. Change of *tenkin*, not only in the ways of implementation, but also in its existence, is called for.

Few people provided me with a solution for this during my fieldwork, except for Mr. Seto below. For him, it is not only companies but also society as a whole that should take this issue of dual-career seekers seriously in the era of labor shortage and then implement better practices to accommodate these couples for Japan's future labor market. As for *tenkin*, he insisted that the practice be abolished.

Negotiating *Tenkin* Itself

I first met Mr. Seto in August 2015, in the course of my fieldwork, seeking companies who would help me conduct interviews. At the time, Mr. Seto was a president of an asset management company, which was one of the subsidiaries of a trading company. I asked him for an-hour interview in his office. In a reception located on an elevator floor, there was a phone, which asked visitors to call an extension number. I called an administrative division, and a woman on the phone told me to enter a meeting room nearby. Soon after, Mr. Seto showed up. This simple way to welcome visitors indicated Mr. Seto's and his firm's pursuit of efficiency.

He was decisive in his opinion about *tenkin* from this very beginning. Right after my introduction, Mr. Seto mentioned that he was unsatisfied with the academic study of *tenkin*. Only a few studies had treated it individually and separately from the whole system, so that they had ended up in making little influence. He rather thought that *tenkin* is a core problem in the employment system and must be eliminated. He insisted that Japanese companies would run a large risk if they continue the *tenkin* system. For him, the *tenkin* system was significantly attributed to a belief that nurturing generalists benefited firms' HR management. But this was a "myth." The belief was only to provide a way out, from his own experience. When he had interacted with executives in foreign firms, he had never encountered such generalists. They had been all specialists, who had no ways to escape from their duties. They should have trod a thorny path and it must have been tough. But without these skills, they would not have been able to boost themselves to such positions, in his opinion.

These thoughts originated from his own experience of *tenkin* that he had undergone while working for the trading company. Three years after he had married his wife, he had been ordered on *tenkin*, as one of the courses that the trading company had usually provided the employees with. It had been soon after their child was born. His wife had had a full-time job so he had wanted to take care of his newly born son together with her. He had not wanted to accept the order. But if he had rejected it, he had to leave his job. The trading company he belonged to at the time had been famous at a model of a TV commercial of an energy drink, whose catch phrase was "Can you fight for twenty-four hours?" In other words, "hierarchy," in his term, had been embedded. White-collar *sarariimen* were supposed to work for the company without thinking about why, let alone asking it. Mr. Seto had been the subject of the *tenkin* system. Eventually, he had flown overseas alone. In the interview with me, Mr. Seto recalled his departure and said, "At the airport, I wept and my heart was broken. I would never want to have such feeling anymore."

Since he came back from the *tenkin*, he had striven to seek a way that he could be promoted without *tenkin* experiences "in THAT trading company," he described. He had even tried to make more profits than those who had been promoted through frequent *tenkin*. Then, he came to understand, if only he made the highest profits in his jobs, no one would have attempted to move him to other posts in which he would probably earn less. As long as he contributed to the profits of the company, no one would complain to him that he had stayed in offices around Tokyo for many years. This was how he was promoted to the president of the subsidiary company. Mr. Seto experienced *tenkin*, negated it, and managed to escape it by exerting agency. His next step was to propagate that the *tenkin* system is only a myth.

He was also determined to critique the social movement to promote the area-based career-track employment scheme. He succinctly mentioned, "The scheme allowed workers to do a job at a lower level." On the other hand, from his experience, he understood that the practice to send someone to some offices both domestically and internationally was necessary for business, more or less, from his managerial point of view. So his ideal solution was to make workers choose which career they want to pursue, specialist type or generalist type. Mr. Seto said:

> If workers chose the former, they might face difficulty in becoming a president of a large company. They could be promoted to managers, though, and it may be enough for most people, I guess. If they prefer the latter, they might need to

experience relocations to learn about management. Yet, in that case, the workers should be given chances to communicate with the boss and HR departments about their thoughts, including timing and location of *tenkin*. This is ideal and fair to me.

The "communication" and "fairness" seemed to be keywords of his life. For him, the "fairness" was not necessarily the sameness, as in the assumption that Ms. Aoi's trading company embodied as I mentioned above. Mr. Seto rather put emphasis on the feeling of understanding which was developed through communication.

Based on these concepts, he had been involved in the activity of a non-profit organization called *Fathering Japan*. The NPO was originally established to promote *ikumen*, or child-caring father. At the time of my fieldwork, Mr. Seto was enthusiastic about another social activity that they called "*ikubosu*," or caring boss, which also aimed to increase *ikumen* and encourage dual-career couples, and for this purpose, strove to pose roles of bosses and managers into question in corporate management. To this end, the organization had held social events nationwide sponsored by local governments. Simultaneously, they attempted to propagate their concept of *ikubosu* to Japanese firms by creating a new social movement of "caring-boss company alliance." By claiming participation in the alliance, Japanese firms could advertise their corporate involvement in the series of activities such as promotions of *ikumen* and dual-career couples. As of April 2024, 271 firms, mostly large and well known, were members (NPO Fathering Japan 2024).

I participated in *Ikubosu* Seminar twice, once in Hiroshima in 2016 and another in Kobe in 2017. The latter seminar, which I elaborate on here, was held over two days. The first day included lectures and group work and lasted three hours. The second-time seminar was held twenty days after the first one for two hours and the same participants reported what they tried in their workplaces after the first seminar. Mr. Seto was a lecturer on both days. Thirty-four participants at the time consisted of government officers of the city of Kobe and employees and HR managers from companies mostly located in the city. After the first-day event, a drinking party was held and almost half of the participants joined and shared their experiences. I applied to participate in the event as a graduate student of Waseda University. Since my affiliation was noted in a list of the participants, I was asked by other participants why I was interested in this seminar. I told them about my research and my desire of learning about their consciousness and reactions toward the seminar.

Messages in the seminar were simple, "Practicing *ikubosu* will benefit your life in the workplace and home." They did not use the word, "work-life balance," because it sounded "lukewarm" to them. Taking advantage of the concept, some workers ended up in a type putting work responsibility onto other workers or only insisting on their rights while doing nothing in their workplaces. So, the lecturers of the seminar including Mr. Seto thought that the concept would not impact business leaders. The concept of *ikubosu* instead emphasized "business results," if not necessarily strongly contributing to them in practice. In order to stimulate the business leaders, the lecturers demonstrated an understanding of the former business environment, in which workers had to devote their whole life to work, while they questioned contemporary working situations, in which many workers had not been able to show full commitment because they were "limited employees." The concept was exemplified by the situation of a baseball team. In a team during the *Shōwa* era, the main players had been "regular" full-time workers who could work whenever and wherever possible. The team also had held a number of such workers on the bench. Nowadays or from now on, however, all of the players have some sort of limitation. They might include workers who were sick, mothers, child-caring fathers, the elderly, foreigners, or single mothers. Also, the team has fewer players waiting to play. Therefore, managing these workers was not optional, but indispensable for corporate management. In this sense, they used the term, efficiency.

In order to achieve this management, however, managers would need to change their mindset to begin with. The sense of "selfless devotion" should be eradicated from their workplace. Rather, they had to send a message that their workers should care for themselves and enrich both their work and life. To this end, managers should try to know what their workers need in their life, including their aspiration for work. For this purpose, managers as well would need to share their own private life with their workers, for them to share theirs easily. This was how the importance of communication came to the fore.

For Mr. Seto, listening to workers was "the first and foremost step on a road map of managers." Otherwise, managers would never know what their workers need. If so, the managers would not be able to rely on their workers to do jobs. As a result, it would not bring profits. On the other hand, if managers kept their doors open, their workers would talk to them at any time about anything. This is a "treasure," according to Mr. Seto. This open-door policy enables the managers to understand which workers they could rely on to do a certain job at a certain time. This would raise profits, and maintain their sense of fairness, or understanding for sharing jobs, among workers, because it would allow them to share their responsibilities in a long run, too. Under the long-term employment system, some workers had more restrictions in certain periods, while others had more in different years. Yet, there was an assumption that no one did only work. It meant that all the workers, including managers, must have something that they could devote themselves to other than work. Having a rest could be included. Otherwise, the fairness would disappear. The assumption and senses of mutual understanding and support should increase the satisfaction of employees, according to the lecturer, which was critical to the role of managers these days.

In practice, too, Mr. Seto was consistent in thinking about workers and thereby achieving corporate interests. For example, if workers had struggles in accomplishing their jobs, it might be caused by lack of time. The shortage, however, was because of "time robbers" such as meetings, email transactions, materials, and hierarchy. He said meetings should be held at minimum times and durations, and for this purpose, materials for meetings should be as simple as possible for the minimum number of participants to be able to read beforehand. The last five minutes of the meetings should be allocated to a "wrap-up time," which could avoid one worker from spending another day for summarizing the minutes. Emails should be "muscular" and light, which meant short, precise, conclusion-first, and with few attachments and addresses. If some important issues were decided in some meetings, managers should ask senior managers to join and make decisions in the same space. Another critical idea in prioritizing workers and corporate efficiency was to choose customers. Mr. Seto suggested severing relationships with those who exhausted workers by saying "no" to their senior bosses and stock holders, too. He believed that these strategies would eventually make more profits for firms. Mr. Seto delivered these messages to participants in the seminars, drawing on his experience several times. This made participants feel a good sense of humor and deliberate about all the issues, overlapping with their own experience. By referring to catchy words from best-selling books such as "hopeless man" and "wives who wish husbands to die," Mr. Seto attempted to stimulate participants, middle-aged managers in particular. Mr. Seto kept saying, "You might have nothing to do at home. YOU must find something to devote yourself to other than work and YOU must leave your office earlier to live a productive life."

Mr. Seto also gave some mention to *tenkin* during the seminar. It was in his suggestion of enhancing communication and fairness. First, managers should deliberate if a certain *tenkin* is necessary, or not. Otherwise, it would maintain its huge cost forever. Yet, if it is necessary, then, they should consider which employees would want the position through open discussion. Otherwise, the fairness, or understanding, of *tenkin* would be instantly questioned. Thus, Mr. Seto emphasized the role of negotiation in the practice of *tenkin*.

All these messages were directed not only to the managers but to workers as well. The lecturers employed a lot of neoliberal adverbs such as subjectively, pro-actively, independently, and voraciously. In other words, not only managers and bosses but also their workers do their jobs in these ways to bring efficiency and more profits to their firms, although all the responsibilities were placed on bosses. The lecturers insisted that bosses support their workers' independence, rather than controlling them.

The participants in the seminar displayed a variety of reactions. In both seminars, they were perhaps aged thirties to fifties, and most of them were HR managers. Around 80 percent were men. On the first day of the Kobe seminar, I participated in a workshop with five other members in one group, and shared experience of each participant and made action plans. Most of them shared their struggles in dealing with their bosses and co-workers and agreed with what consumes their time, their waste of time in emails and meetings in particular. Giving understanding to the concept of *ikubosu*, they discussed how they could spread the concept in their workplaces and also how they could incorporate it into their private lives, as well. In the after-seminar drinking party, too, they willingly and enjoyably shared their experiences and listened to those of others. It was a site of inter-company interactions. In the second seminar, however, where the participants were supposed to review their problems at their workplaces, some of them were active, while others were not. The activists challenged their plans in the workplace. For example, one man had endeavored to join a lunch party where all others had been female workers, trying to understand their private situations more. Another man had cut the number and length of meetings. On the other hand, one woman shared difficulty in setting a KPI (Key Performance Indicator), thereby she gained less understanding and support from her colleagues than she imagined. Another man, who worked in the financial sector, expressed disappointment in his uncooperative workplace culture. He commented that his senior managers were incapable of imagining a link between *ikubosu* and corporate interests. Also, he had been swamped with his own work and not been able to find time for the activity. Mr. Seto showed understanding to the corporate culture of the firm, and criticized the senior managers, saying that they should have to take the seminar. In all these cases, the participants learned their own ways, more or less, to show legitimacy in challenging the dominant norms in their workplaces and homes and thereby to challenge cultural and gendered boundaries between the public and domestic spheres through negotiation.

SIGNS OF CHANGE

My participatory observation in the *Ikubosu* Seminar was crucial in my study of *tenkin* for the following reasons: First, the activists, including Mr. Seto, were decisive. They knew that the concepts they were propagating were meaningful from their own experience, and it would be significant to others and society on the whole, too. Second, the activists could be role models. They were middle-aged men of dual-career couples who worked for companies as managers which were familiar to many people. They succeeded in having participants compare the attitudes of these activists with those of themselves as managers or those sitting near the participants in their everyday workplaces. Third, they tried to solve the work-life conflicts of the participants collaboratively in flat interactions. It was influential that the participants learned how to incorporate their private life into the public space, crossing the boundary. Most of the participants had multiple roles as managers, workers, spouses, and parents. They struggled in balancing their work and private lives every day, so only dealing with one issue did not work to solve the other. It was indispensable for them to discuss the issues thoroughly and frankly. Fourth, in both workplace and home, including through the practice of *tenkin*, the activists encouraged the negotiation of actors in conventional environments as an art of bringing about change. They did not thrust self-responsibility arguments onto individual workers who were usually at the bottom of the hierarchy. They clearly claimed that it should be these workers' bosses in the middle or higher level of the hierarchy who should be responsible for the workers' fair achievements in their work, as well as in their family lives. To put it otherwise, they called into question the conventional power and gendered relationships in workplaces and tried to overcome them through people's agency, especially those of the managers. Last, the activity not only developed the participants' own agency. It also fostered hopes for other people nearby to become capable of negotiating cultural and gendered norms. The activists in the *Ikubosu* Seminar played all in all, what Antonio Gramsci (Giuseppe 1970) called, the role of the organic intellectuals. Their challenges to the conventional employment practices such as long working hours and *tenkin* were influencing.

In February 2018, there was a news report regarding *tenkin* (Sankei Shimbun 2018). One general insurance firm, a member of the caring-boss company alliance since 2015 (NPO Fathering Japan 2024), has abolished *tenkin* as a requirement for career-track workers. The firm has newly created thirteen areas for domestic transfers and the workers are transferred within the area. They have plans to do the trial in two areas from July 2018, and hoped to expand the system to all 7,000 career-track workers by January, 2019. The same article on Sankei Shimbun (2018) mentioned the firm's purpose for this change as an attempt to accommodate its dual-career couples as well as elder-caring workers who are increasing these days. By boosting its reputation as a "good-place-to-work" company, the firm then aims to hire and secure "good, skilled" workers from the labor market, which is shrinking, and therefore, in which these financial firms will face severer competition. Mr. Seto also introduced the news report in his email magazine, extolling the firm's courage and efforts, or agencies of the HR managers, in making this challenge for the change.

During the COVID pandemic, while online working styles became common, a news article (Yomiuri Shimbun 2021) reported that one nationwide company decided to abolish *tenkin* and shift the working style to the one that workers can fulfill their well-being. Whether or not such movements will be accomplished and also become mainstream, it is now obvious that some companies question the efficiencies of *tenkin*, the mandatory transfers. I also hear from neighbors that, let alone *tenkin*, some IT companies let their employees work full remote. One of the reasons for the shift was serious labor shortage in the industry. In such companies, *tenkin* is not anymore taken for granted.

As this chapter showed, although the samples were few, there were signs of change in *tenkin* to more flexible, gender-equal practices. Some workers in this study made *tenkin* and its related practices become negotiable. They indicated that it is workers themselves, not only the government and employers, that also maneuver their careers to the better.

NOTES

1. Such a practice also seemed to be employed by other firms, according to my interviewees, although they commonly had little idea of its purposes and functions.

2. The term *ikumen* here seemed to be employed in the same contexts discussed in North (2014). The term had positive connotations for the women I interviewed, because it seemed to suggest contributions to their daily lives as well as to society.

3. One can remember that the description, *chūzai*, was used by job-hunting students at university, as I mentioned in chapter 3. It has become obvious how the term played a part of a discourse of overseas *tenkin*, not only from workers' but also from families' point of view.

4. She also took authorized nursery center [*ninshō hoikujo*] into consideration, which was run by the prefectural government of Tokyo, but she did not like the environment there, where her daughter might spend all day in one room of a building.

5. According to the Ministry of Health, Labor, and Welfare, the proportion of utilization of paid leaves is 49.4 percent (MHLW 2017b). This data means, although employees are given 18.2-day paid leaves a year per person on average, they tend to take only a half, nine days, of them. The rate differs, depending on which industry the employees belong to, for example, electric, gas, and water utilities mark the highest rate, 71.8 percent, while hotels, restaurants, and leisure services mark the lowest, 32.8 percent.

6. Cases in which a fear and uncertainty became a catalyst for marriage also attracted attention after 3/11 Great Tohoku Earthquake in 2011, and were also shared by my other informants.

7. As I described in chapter 2 with explanation by the vice president, Mr. Tsuchida, Motomachi's promotion exam consists of general appraisals, a written exam, and interview, and is held once a year. With the efforts of the multiple screenings, Mr. Tsuchida said that the company tries to strictly select the right person in the right timing.

Conclusion
Career Management in Contemporary Japan

Japanese society has shown various signs of moving toward a transition recently, including the acceleration of demographic change and ensuing labor shortage, delay in marriage and childbirth or withdrawal from both, and diversification of actors in the labor market. These actors include dual-career households. Both the government and business world have sought ways to accommodate more and more female workers, by adopting various policies and systems. Most recently in 2022, the amended Act on the Promotion of Women's Active Engagement in Professional Life stipulates that Japanese companies with 301 employees or more are required to disclose their gender pay gap (MHLW 2022). The society is in transition.

Tenkin is one of the employment practices that has attracted more and more attention lately. A governmental committee (MHLW 2017a) notes that *tenkin* hinders women's work-life balance and therefore requires firms to consider these women's family situations. Academic studies using lenses of gender (Kurotani 2005; Connor 2010), too, have argued the inequality that the practice has caused. The government and its committee have stressed the necessity of the model shift from *Shōwa* to *Reiwa* and treated *tenkin* as an issue (Nagase 2022). To boost the proportion of female managers, a change in the practice has been called for.

Amidst these social dynamics, I conducted this study of *Tenkin in Employment and Family*. Over three years between 2014 and 2017, I interviewed HR managers of large Japanese firms and individual white-collar dual-career couples, who conducted and experienced *tenkin*, respectively. I also observed several social events that had a relation to the practice of *tenkin* and explored the discourse of the practice. In addition, I reviewed previous research regarding transfers and *tenkin* in Japanese employment and family structures, aiming to understand the practice more deeply. Thus, I conducted research on *tenkin* across time and space.

The umbrella questions I sought to answer were as follows: How on earth was *tenkin* produced? How do firms implement the practice of *tenkin* in contemporary workplace and also deal with the employees who have *tenkin* and the practice of *tenkin*? If there are any practices that individual workers play, what are they and what consciousness do the actors have? Then, what outcomes do their actions bring about? Finally, how should *tenkin* evolve? For the conceptual framework, I particularly employed Sherry Ortner's (2006) views on structure and agency, which put emphasis on the orientation that human beings are inherently motivated to seek the better in their everyday living, shape desires and strive for intentions according to culturally constituted repertories in diverse ways.

PRODUCTION OF *TENKIN*

Tenkin was produced historically. Historical records and postwar empirical studies demonstrate that *tenkin* has its roots in Japan's cultural and gendered labor market structure. The practice existed in the *Edo* period, where the Internal Labor Markets, the rationale for *tenkin*, were seen. Around that time, *tenkin* was adopted by various firms mainly for the purposes of training and promotion. The practice became dominant in the postwar *Shōwa* era, along with the establishment and development of the ILM in Japan. In the late 1940s, when heavy labor disputes occurred in manufacturing, these firms made choices to retain their blue-collar workers by transfers, rather than to dismiss them, for financial reasons. By calculating the costs in both practices, these employers found that transfer was more efficient. Although the workers were concerned about forging new lives in different cities, they had to accept *tenkin*, since it was their only choice to maintain their quality of life which was about to deteriorate during the immediate postwar period. Associated with a shift in labor relations, *tenkin* for white-collar workers also became dominant as a purposeful practice. It was not only for training and promotion but also for HR development under long-term employment security. Since then, *tenkin* has been conducted as common sense both for employers and employees as one reasonable practice in Japan's ILM.

Socioeconomic studies have argued that the establishment of this common sense regarding *tenkin* is attributed to people's behavior in Japanese workplaces. For instance, the customary meaning of a "job" is obscure among workers, so transfers between jobs are more easily accepted. This can contribute to frequent, periodic *tenkin*. Or, a norm of a community where workers seek common interests inside a firm and also compete with each other under a seniority-based merit system has helped them foster a sense of efficiency in the practice of *tenkin*. Furthermore, Japanese courts have contributed to maintaining the norm of compulsory *tenkin*.

I argue that, in addition to the functions just mentioned, the gender division of labor has helped to sustain *tenkin* as legitimate. The male-breadwinner and female-full-time-homemaker model enables *tenkin* to function. Women follow their husbands on *tenkin*, or women send their husbands alone to *tenkin* by *tanshin funin*, and thereby, they take full care of domestic responsibilities for the husbands. This has hindered some working women from fulfilling their careers through *tenkin*, both their own and their husbands', which has allowed the gendered structures of *tenkin*, as well as the workplaces in Japan, to be reinforced. Thus, my review of previous literature has uncovered the cultural normative, gendered feature of *tenkin* as a crucial practice in Japan's labor market.

TRANSFORMATION OF *TENKIN*?

The firms I interviewed dealt with *tenkin* as taken for granted. They believed and insisted that *tenkin* contributes to their workers' HR development and firms' efficiency. *Tenkin* embodies various purposes, such as training and skill development, and the custom helps them function smoothly. These factors are the constituents of the ILM, conducive to the efficient running of the firms. And people in the firms take it for granted, as their gendered assumptions in combination with the custom make sense of them. The implementation of *tenkin* by contemporary Japanese firms is reproduced by capitalists' logic and gendered family assumptions which are now embedded in the whole society.

Yet the research also revealed that some firms attempted to lead change in their HR management including *tenkin*. First, the series of reforms were initiated by employees themselves, including the company union and working groups. This helped the employers review the effects of *tenkin*, and thereby, the practice of *tenkin* itself. In so doing, the employers adopted the concept of diversity and inclusion, with the mind that the more female workers they attempted to include in managerial positions, the more diversified the workplace became, and the more innovative ideas the companies could pursue in their global competitions. There, negotiable labor-management relations were being built, although the practice ended up being held hierarchically, with employers maintaining the upper hand. Behind these personnel changes, there was the impact of the global economy. Lately, since these manufacturers were required to compete in the severe global business environment, they needed to make their workers play active roles in it, by making full use of their job skills, languages, as well as human capabilities. In this context, their changes might be also driven by these larger economic forces.

As a result, these firms also had difficulties in fully incorporating into managerial positions those female workers who had family responsibility. Through the process, indeed, various tensions arose one after another, between genders or within one gender. Legal statutes and negotiation were insufficient to transform firms toward a gender-equal model. These examples laid bare that *tenkin* as well as the gender role structure that underpins it is thus firmly embedded still in Japan's contemporary employment structure.

EVOLVING DUAL-CAREER COUPLES

The couples I interviewed were constrained by this structure but at the same time substantially happiness seekers. Pursuing careers were, for them, means to achieve their lifework. The women had few options to become full-time homemakers. Some learned a lesson from their own experience in which they had taken a year of childcare leave and been bored doing nothing every day. For these women, engagement in their work was fulfillment in their lives.

Thus when they had their *tenkin* or their spouses' *tenkin*, they negotiated with their spouses at home, as well as with various people at the workplace. The matters they had to bring up were diverse, including their house, children's daycare center, baby sitter, and systems to allow them take leave. These institutions served as their resources, helped them construct new subjectivities for moving forward, and take new actions toward the practice of *tenkin*. There, they guided their work and family lives according to their desires, which were determined by their "local logics of the good and the desirable and how to pursue them" (Ortner 2006).

Through the negotiation, moreover, the workers influence each other. They not only listened to what the other people said, but also came to monitor reflexively what they had done and would have to do, as Giddens describes it "practical consciousness" (Giddens 1979: 24). Then, they articulated their intentions, with inherent capabilities to seek better lives and also careful adaption to conventional repertoires of their structures. In so doing, they changed the meanings of the conventional practices and adopted the changes in interactions with others across the structures, between family and employment, of other societies and cultures as well in the cases of overseas *tenkin*. There, various resources, if not visible, were invoked in their relationships. In family, while seeking independence and support from their spouses, the couples developed flexible mindsets and attitudes toward their family lives. As a result, these people transposed the conventional practices in their homes, in the ways that Ortner (1984, 2006) manifests, if not the drastic change in the gendered social system. The dual-career couples in this study showed that they could live apart with economic independence and also collaborate with each other for their career aspirations. Their mothering roles tended to remain mostly at their hand, as they had no choice when either of the couple had *tenkin* suddenly, and also because they think they are required by their children who are socialized in Japan. Yet, their decisions were made as a consequence of negotiation with their spouses and in themselves.

NEED FOR LABOR MARKET REFORM

Now that Japanese dual-career couples are evolving and many Japanese firms are craving to hire and secure good, skilled workers due to the shrinking labor market, the cultural normative, gendered practice of *tenkin* should be eliminated. This would not necessarily entail eradication of inter-regional transfer. *Tenkin* should become the sort of corporate transfer that is usually conducted in enterprises of other countries or other types of labor markets. For example, in a British company for which I used to work during my *tenkin*, employees were usually asked by employers if they were willing or not for a certain transfer. Even for a short-term business trip, workers were provided such options, and it was not a problem, even if they declined the offer. More precisely, *tenkin* should not be ordered, but be negotiated. It should not be utilized as the alternative form of dismissal or as a kind of harassment.

In the first place, the government should delete the stipulation of *tenkin*, the mandatory transfers, from its model work rules book Clause 8, 3 (MHLW 2023: 14). As we saw in chapter 1, Clause 8, 1 and 2 stipulates that transfers "may" (MHLW 2023: 14) be ordered. Because it leaves uncertainty, employees should also remain uncertain to the offer of any transfers, even though they have no "good reason" (MHLW 2023: 14), whose meaning is also vague and should depend on each firm's custom. Furthermore, the model work rules book specifies Clause 8, 3 is only applied to Clause 8, 2 of *shukkō* cases, but many workers believe in a robust norm such that they feel they cannot reject any transfers, as my qualitative study indicated.

In addition, I suggest that transfers be voluntary. It is obvious that, from my own experience as well, transfer plays a certain role in developing workers' experiences and skills. As this study implies, however, voluntary transfers can contribute to enhancing their job capabilities more efficiently. Also, if they have clear information about when, where, for how long, and why they are transferred, their HR development may advance with clearer time scales. There, a space for mutual communication and negotiation across positions in their hierarchical systems is needed, so that both employers and employees can reach an understanding of what they are required to do while enhancing fairness among workers. In such a new practice of inter-regional corporate transfer, roles that the bosses and managers take are substantial. In any social situation, matching is difficult but both employers and employees will need to try harder to achieve better, more rational and more equitable implementation of corporate transfers.

I also suggest that abolishment of inter-regional transfer itself be taken into consideration. For this to happen, the conditions of the Internal Labor Market would need to be more flexible. In the market, transfer is given too many purposes, such as training, promotion, and HR development. In financial industries, in addition, transfer functions to prevent white-collar crimes. Yet, I want to question, is it impossible to meet these purposes without workers' mandatory relocations? Does OJT have to include compulsory transfer lasting for a long period? Do firm-specific skills as well as long-term employment truly benefit employees and employers in contemporary society? How much do we, the workers, have to rely on a labor market mechanism which was developed many decades ago? Compared to the past market, as this study has indicated, business is more global and actors of the market are more diverse, while their working conditions are more restricted. A new style of a labor market is called for in *Reiwa* Japan.

The labor market transition can be more or less led by the transformation of labor relations driven by interpersonal negotiation, as a complement to weakened collective bargaining power by Japanese corporate unions. In the Internal Labor Market, under the long-term employment system, capitalists with the card of dismissal always outweigh the power of labor. In *tenkin*, moreover, because of its embodiment of custom and gender, male workers are more prone to be the subjects of exploitation by their male employers. However, if individual workers strive to acquire various resources and build relationships with new actors, as this study suggests, they can strengthen their labor power and negotiate their employment practices.

Yet, it has to be remembered that such negotiation can be a double-edged sword. For example, if negotiation is conducted in closed spaces by less-empowered workers in terms of educational success, socialization, physical condition, or language ability, the practice may function to make such workers more and more vulnerable to their employers' art of power. Therefore, interpersonal negotiation in the workplace could serve merely as a pillar of bargaining power. Collective power should not be undermined. These double attacks may help to transform the labor market to one more compatible with people in contemporary Japanese society.

RECONSIDERING "CAREER" IN JAPAN'S CONTEXTS

Last but not least, I would like to stress, through this study of career management of dual-career couples, the importance of reviewing the senses of "career" in Japanese contexts from two perspectives. In the concluding remarks in chapter 3, I discussed the meaning of "career" in Japan. I argued that the imported word, "career," may induce workers to see a good prospect of taking advantage of their work and life. But in the Japanese ILM, it is impossible for workers to do so. Their life is more or less, or for better or worse, at the hand of their employers, as the study uncovered. So it is a misunderstanding that career can be built on a worker's discretion in Japan.

The second aspect, which the study clarified and therefore I want to emphasize here, is that the concept of "career" must include the workers' private realm from the gender perspective, the senses of care in particular. Eva Feder Kittay (1999) puts that "we are all interdependent" (Kittay 1999: xii). This study revealed that while workers are promoted through *tenkin*, they have been more or less dependent on somebody who does care for the workers, either transferees or their spouses. No one is living without their own care or somebody's care. The care is essential in the workplace, family, community, or nationally. If it comes to *tenkin* for dual-career couples, who have to be separated due to *tenkin* but tend to seek to "have it all," the care dependency is put into practice as almost taken for granted. But no one mentioned this point to me during the interview. The society lacks the sense of care in the concept of career. The lenses of gender and care should be incorporated in the discussion of career management. Thus, the meaning of career is not limited to the career-track workers, but open to all workers.

As Kittay (1999) discusses, we are all equally in need of care for our own and others. In *Reiwa* era, the Japanese context of "career" has to embrace the management of both work and private life. That is, career management should mean to manage both work and private life. With this in mind, it is imperative to reform the *Shōwa* practice of *tenkin*.

Appendix A
The Firms Interviewed by the Author

Appendix A

Table A.1 The Firms Interviewed by the Author

	Motomachi	Tachibana	Kamisato	Okamoto	Hiroo	Mizuki	Satomura
Industry	Manufacturer (electronic devices)	Newspaper company	Manufacturer (components for industrial machinery and automobiles)	General insurance firm	Manufacturer (machines for food production)	Manufacturer (lingerie)	Manufacturer (pharmaceutical products, cosmetics and foods)
Date(s) of interview	Jul. 30, 2015 Feb. 9, 2017	Dec. 14, 2015	Dec. 15, 2015	Jan. 18, 2016	Mar. 24, 2016	Feb. 3, 2017	Feb. 3, 2017
Interviewees	Vice President HR manager HR manager	HR vice-director HR manager Editorial writer	HR manager Section chief	HR manager	HR manager	HR manager HR manager HR staff	HR staff
Approx. number of employees (individual)	7,000	2,500	7,000	20,000	1,000	5,000	1,000
Approx. number of those who have tenkin	4,000	2,500	3,000	5,000	750	Unknown	Unknown
Employment category	Career track	Regular	Career track	All area	Global	Career track	Career track
Frequency of tenkin	Depends on business need	Depends on person	Depends on business need	Every 5–6 years	Depends on business need	Depends on business need	Depends on business need
Purposes for tenkin	HR development	Appropriate deployment Career development	HR development	Career development Private reasons	Appropriate deployment	HR development	Unknown
System	Following leave	Reemployment	None	None	None	Reemployment	None
Ratio of female managers* (%)	2	N/A	2	2	17	21	16
Ratio of newly-entering career-track female workers* (%)	4	50	13	6	19	56	39

Source: Generated by the Author.
* The data were from Corporate Quarterly Report for Recruitment (Toyo Keizai Shinposha, 2014), unless I came to know during the interviews.

Appendix B
The Individuals Interviewed by the Author

Table B.1   Seventeen Female Workers Who Experienced Their Own *Tenkin*

Pseudonym	Ms. Sakura	Ms. Enami	Ms. Nonaka	Ms. Ota	Ms. Uchida
Date(s) of interview	Jun. 06, 2015	Jun. 20, 2015	Jul. 12, 2015	Aug. 12, 2015	Aug. 19, 2015
Affiliation	Newspaper company	Travel agency	Manufacturer	Airline company	News agency
Type of employment	Writer	Operation	Specialist	Non-career-track worker	Writer
Age	38	42	27	46	32
Where she had *tenkin*	Hyogo / Aichi	France / Tokyo	Miyagi	Tokyo	Oita / Niigata / Miyagi
Husband's affiliation	Construction company	Manufacturer	Trading company	Airport company	National Government
Where he had *tenkin*	Osaka	Tokyo			Oita / Saga
Number of child(ren)	0	1	0	0	1

Pseudonym	Ms. Hino	Ms. Narita	Ms. Aoi	Ms. Kawano	Ms. Matsunaga
Date(s) of interview	Sep. 29, 2015	Oct. 15, 2015	Nov. 10, 2015	Nov. 17, 2015	Dec. 21, 2015
Age	39	30	35	43	32
Affiliation	Manufacturer	Manufacturer	Trading company	Financial firm	Newspaper company
Type of employment	Career-track employee	Career-track employee	Career-track employee	Career-track employee	Writer
Where she had *tenkin*	Tokyo / China	Shiga	United States	Ibaraki / Aomori	Nara
Husband's affiliation	Manufacturer	Manufacturer	Trading company	Government	Television station
Where he had *tenkin*	Tokyo	Okayama	United States	Ibaraki / Aomori	
Number of child(ren)	2	1	3	2	2

Appendix B   147

Pseudonym	Ms. Baba	Ms. Harada	Ms. Mikami	Ms. Inoue	Ms. Komine
Date(s) of interview	Jan. 14, 2016	Jan. 19, 2016	Jan. 25, 2016	Jan. 31, 2016	Feb. 01, 2016
Age	33	34	32	39	37
Affiliation	Manufacturer	Manufacturer	General insurance firm	College	National Government
Type of employment	Career-track employee	Career-track employee	Career-track employee	Lecturer	Career-track employee
Where she had *tenkin*	Singapore	Okayama	Shizuoka	Aomori	Aichi
Husband's affiliation	Manufacturer	Manufacturer	General insurance firm	Government	General insurance firm
Where he had *tenkin*	Shiga	Ibaraki	Miyagi		Aichi
					Brazil
Number of child(ren)	1	2	1	0	1

Pseudonym	Ms. Hosaka	Ms. Katano
Date(s) of interview	May 16, 2016	Feb. 14, 2017
Age	43	50
Affiliation	Newspaper company	IT consulting firm
Type of employment	Writer	Career-track employee
Where she had *tenkin*	Nagano	Kanagawa
Husband's affiliation	Newspaper company	N/A
Where he had *tenkin*	United States	Tokyo
	United States	
Number of child(ren)	2	1

Source: Generated by the Author.

Appendix B

Table B.2 Five Male Workers Who Experienced Their Own *Tenkin*

Pseudonym	Mr. Takahara	Mr. Kaji	Mr. Hayashi	Mr. Sakura	Mr. Maruyama
Date(s) of interview	Dec. 23, 2014	Feb. 08, 2015	Mar. 04, 2015	Jul. 06, 2015	Oct. 24, 2015
Age	36	36	39	39	34
Affiliation	National government	General insurance firm	Railway company	Construction company	Manufacturer
Type of employment	Non-career-track official	Career-track employee	Career-track employee	Career-track employee	Career-track employee
Where he had tenkin	Tokyo Osaka Tokyo	Kagoshima Ishikawa Hiroshima	Tokyo Hiroshima	Osaka	Ibaraki Aomori
Wife's affiliation	General Insurance firm	Temporary staff agency	Manufacturer	Newspaper company	Manufacturer
Where she had tenkin				Hyogo Aichi	
Number of child(ren)	3	1	2	0	0

Source: Generated by the Author.

Appendix B   149

Table B.3 Twenty-Three Female Workers and One Male Worker Who Only Experienced Their Husbands' or his Wife's *Tenkin*

Pseudonym	Ms. Takahara	Ms. Fukushima	Ms. Kaji	Ms. Komatsu	Ms. Morii
Date(s) of interview	Dec. 01, 2014; Dec. 23, 2014; Oct. 19, 2015	Jan. 28, 2015; May 27, 2015	Jan. 28, 2015; Feb. 08, 2015; Jul. 01, 2015	Mar. 26, 2015	May 26, 2015
Age	36	45	36	42	40
Affiliation	General insurance firm	Temporary staff agency	Temporary staff agency	Manufacturer	Private school
Type of employment	Area-based worker	Dispatched worker	Semi-regular worker	Non-career-track worker	Teacher
Husband's affiliation	National government	General Insurance	General Insurance	Manufacturer	Manufacturer
Where he had *tenkin*	Hiroshima Osaka	Tokyo Hokkaido Okayama Hokkaido Hiroshima	Ishikawa Hiroshima	Taiwan	United Kingdom United Arab Emirates Vietnam
Number of child(ren)	3	0	1	2	2

Pseudonym	Ms. Maruyama	Ms. Honda	Ms. Tabata	Ms. Hayashi	Ms. Shimura
Date(s) of interview	Jul. 12, 2015	Jul. 12, 2015	Jul. 13, 2015	Jul. 18, 2015	Jul. 28, 2015
Age	34	36	34	37	34
Affiliation	Manufacturer	Manufacturer	Construction company	Manufacturer	Local bank
Type of employment	Career-track worker	Career-track worker	Area-based worker	Company nurse	Career-track worker
Husband's affiliation	Manufacturer	Manufacturer	Travel agency	Railway company	Newspaper company
Where he had tenkin	Aomori	Malaysia Osaka	United States (Guam)	Tokyo Hiroshima	Kumamoto Nagasaki Aichi
Number of child(ren)	0	1	1	2	0

(*Continued*)

Table B.3 (Continued)

Pseudonym	Ms. Yokokawa	Ms. Tokachi	Ms. Okazaki	Ms. Tomosaka	Ms. Kai
Date(s) of interview	Aug. 01, 2015	Aug. 03, 2015	Aug. 04, 2015	Aug. 06, 2015	Aug. 07, 2015
Age	40	33	36	41	41
Affiliation	Manufacturer	Human resource service	Prefecture	Airline company	Advertising company
Type of employment	Career-track worker	Career-track worker	Teacher	Contract worker	Career-track worker
Husband's affiliation	Television station	Telecommunications	Prefecture	Manufacturer	Trading company
Where he had tenkin	S. Korea	United States	Malaysia	Okayama	Miyagi
Number of child(ren)	3	0	2	1	1

Pseudonym	Ms. Umemori	Ms. Taga	Ms. Nakai	Ms. Kamiya	Ms. Kataoka
Date(s) of interview	Aug. 08, 2015	Aug. 11, 2015	Oct. 06, 2015	Oct. 13, 2015	Dec. 01, 2015
Age	33	34	42	36	32
Affiliation	Bank	Medical center	Government	University	General insurance firm
Type of employment	Area-based worker	Social worker	Official	Lecturer	Career-track worker
Husband's affiliation	Bank	News agency	Government	Advertising company	General insurance
Where he / she had tenkin	Osaka	Nagano	United States	Aichi	Hyogo
Number of child(ren)	0	1	4	1	2

Pseudonym	Ms. Ikeda	Ms. Yamabe	Ms. Akitaya	Mr. Nonaka
Date(s) of interview	Dec. 31, 2015	Jan. 19, 2016	Jan. 29, 2016	Jul. 12, 2015
Age	41	33	30	29
Affiliation	Television station	Trading company	Temporary staff agency	Trading company
Type of employment	Career-track worker	Career-track worker	Non-career-track worker	Career-track worker
Husband's affiliation	Manufacturer	Trading company	Government	Manufacturer
Where he / she had tenkin	Canada	Brazil	Hiroshima	Miyagi
		Singapore	Hiroshima	
Number of child(ren)	2	2	1	0

Source: Generated by the Author.

Bibliography

Araki, Takashi. 2011. "The Widening Gap between Standard and Non-standard Employees and the Role of Labor Law in Japan." *University of Tokyo Journal of Law and Politics* 8: 3–19.

Aronsson, Anne S. 2012. *Career Women in Contemporary Japan: Pursuing Identities, Fashioning Lives*. PhD Dissertation. Yale University.

Bourdieu, Pierre. 2001. *Masculine Domination*. Stanford: Stanford University Press.

———. 1977. *Outline of a Theory of Practice*. Cambridge: Cambridge University Press.

Cabinet Office. 2016. "Booklet for The New Support System for Children and Childrearing", accessed Sep. 30, 2023, https://www8.cao.go.jp/shoushi/shinseido/event/publicity/naruhodo_book_2804.html.

Cole, Robert E. 1979. *Work, Mobility, and Participation: A Comparative Study of American and Japanese Industry*. Berkeley: University of California Press.

Connor, Blaine Phillip. 2010. *Transfers and Private Lives of Public Servants in Japan: Teachers in Nagasaki's Outer Islands*. Ph.D. Dissertation. University of Pittsburgh, Pennsylvania.

Dalton, Emma, and Laura Dales. 2016. "Online Konkatsu and the Gendered Ideals of Marriage in Contemporary Japan." *Japanese Studies* 36 (1): 1–19.

Doeringer, Peter B., and Michael J. Piore. 1971. *Internal Labor Markets and Manpower Analysis*. Lexington; Massachusetts: Health.

Dore, Ronald P. 1973. *British Factory-Japanese Factory: The Origins of National Diversity in Industrial Relations*. Berkley, Los Angels: University of California Press.

Edwards, Walter. 1989. *Modern Japan through Its Weddings: Gender Person, and Society in Ritual Portrayal*. Stanford, California: Stanford University Press.

Emerson, Robert M., Rachel I. Fretz, and Linda L. Shaw. 2001. "Participant Observation and Fieldnotes." In Paul Atkinson, Amanda Coffrey, Sara Delamont, John Lofland, and Lyn Lofland eds., *Handbook of Ethnography,* 352–68. London: Sage.

Gender Equality Bureau. 2023. *Danjo kyōdō sankaku hakusho* [White Paper on Gender Equality], assessed Sep. 30, 2023, https://www.gender.go.jp/about_danjo/whitepaper/r05/zentai/pdf/r05_tokusyu.pdf.

———. 2015. *Danjo kyōdō sankaku hakusho* [White Paper on Gender Equality], accessed Sep. 30, 2023, http://www.gender.go.jp/about_danjo/whitepaper/h27/zentai/html/honpen/b1_s06_01.html.

Giddens, Anthony. 1979. *Central Problems in Social Theory: Action, Structure and Contradiction in Social Analysis*. Berkley; Los Angels: University of California Press.

Giuseppe, Fiori. 1970. *Antonio Gramsci: Life of a Revolutionary Translated by Tom Nairn*. NYC: Schocken Books.

Goldstein-Gidoni, Ofra. 2012. *Housewives of Japan: An Ethnography of Real Lives and Consumerized Domesticity*. New York: Palgrave Macmillan.

Gordon, Andrew D. 2012. *Nihon rōshi kankei shi* [The History of Labor Relations in Japan]. Tokyo: Iwanami shoten.

———. 1985. *The Evolution of Labor Relations in Japan: Heavy Industry, 1853–1955*. Cambridge, Massachusetts, Council on East Asian Studies, Harvard University: University of Harvard Press.

Hamaguchi, Keiichirō. 2011. *Nihon no koyō to rōdōhō* [Japanese Employment and Labor Law]. Tokyo: Nihon keizai shinbun shuppan sha.

Hatvany, Nina, and Vladimir Pucik. 1981. "An Integrated Management System: Lessons from the Japanese Experience." *Academy of Management Review* 6 (3): 469–80.

Ishii-Kuntz, Masako. 2003. "Balancing Fatherhood and Work: Emergence of Diverse Masculinities in Contemporary Japan." In Roberson, James E., and Nobue Suzuki eds., *Men and Masculinities in Contemporary Japan: Dislocating the Salaryman Doxa*, 198–216. London: Routledge Curzon.

———. 1995. "Parental Involvement and Perception toward Fathers' Roles: A Comparison between Japan and the United States." In Marsiglio, William ed., *Fatherhood: Contemporary Theory, Research, and Social Policy*, 102–17. Thousand Oaks, California: Sage Publications.

JILPT [Japan Institute for Labor Policy and Training]. 2017. *Kigyō ni okeru tenkin no jittai ni kansuru chōsa chōsa kekka no gaiyō* [Summary of Research Result on Situations of *Tenkin* in Corporations], accessed Sep. 30, 2023, http://www.jil.go.jp/event/ro_forum/20170629/resume/02-chosa-ogino.pdf.

Kim, Young. 2008. "Personnel Management Reforms in Japanese Supermarkets: The Positional Warfare and Limited Assimilation of Conversational Communities." *Social Science Japan Journal* 11 (2): 183–99.

Kittay, Eva Feder. 2020 [1999]. *Love's Labor: Essays on Women, Equality and Dependency*. New York and London: Routledge.

Klien, Susanne. 2021. "Japan's Younger Generations Look for a New Way of Living." *Current History* 120 (827): 240–5.

Koike, Kazuo. 1997. *Nihon kigyō no jinzai keisei: Fukakujitsusei ni taiousuru tameno nouhau* [Personnel Development in Japanese Companies: Knowhow to Deal with Uncertainty]. Tokyo: Chūō kōronsha.

———. 1991. *Daisotsu howaito karā no jinzai kaihatsu* [Personnel Development for College-graduate White-collar Workers]. Tokyo: Tōyō keizai shinpōsha.
Krogness, Karl Jakob. 2011. "The Ideal, the Deficient, and the Illogical Family: An Initial Typology of Administrative Household Units." In Ronald, Richard, and Allison Alexy eds., *Home and Family in Japan: Continuity and Transformation*, 65–90. Milton Park, Abingdon, Oxon, and New York: Routledge.
Kumazawa, Makoto. 1989. *Nihonteki Keiei no Meian* [Light and Dark Outcome of Japanese Employment]. Tokyo: Chikuma Shobō.
Kurotani, Sawa. 2005. *Home away from Home: Japanese Corporate Wives in the United States*. Durham, NC: Duke University Press.
Lam, Alice. 1993. "Equal Employment Opportunities for Japanese Women: Changing Company Practice." In Hunter, Janet ed., *Japanese Women Working*, 197–223. London: Routledge.
———. 1992. *Women and Japanese Management: Discrimination and Reform*. London: Routledge.
Lebra, Takie Sugiyama. 1984. *Japanese Women: Constraint and Fulfillment*. Honolulu: University of Hawaii Press.
Mackie, Vera. 2002. "Embodiment, Citizenship, and Social Policy in Contemporary Japan." In Goodman, Roger ed., *Family and Social Policy in Japan: Anthropological Approaches*, 200–29. Cambridge: Cambridge University press.
Mathews, Gordon. 2014. "Being a Man in a Straitened Japan: The View from Twenty Years Later." In Kawano, Satsuki, Glenda S. Roberts, and Susan Orpett Long eds., *Capturing Contemporary Japan: Differentiation and Uncertainty*, 60–80. Honolulu: University of Hawaii Press.
———. 2004. "Seeking a Career, Finding a Job: How Young People Enter and Resist the Japanese World of Work." In Mathews, Gordon, and Bruce White eds., *Japan's Changing Generations: Are young People Creating a New Society?*, 121–36. London: Routledge.
———. 2003. "Can 'a Real Man' Live for his Family? Ikigai and Masculinity in Today's Japan." In Roberson, James E., and Nobue Suzuki eds., *Men and Masculinities in Contemporary Japan: Dislocating the Salaryman Doxa*, 109–25. London: Routledge Curzon.
Meguro, Yoriko, and Shibata Hirotoshi. 1999. *"Kigyō shugi to kazoku"* [Corporate-centered Society and Family]. In Meguro, Yoriko, and Watanabe Hideaki eds., *Kōza Shakaigaku II Kazoku* [Lecture Sociology II Family], 59–87. Tokyo: University of Tokyo Press.
MHLW [Ministry of Health, Labor, and Welfare]. 2023. *"Moderu shūgyō kisoku"* [A Model Work Rules Book], accessed Sep. 30, 2023, https://www.mhlw.go.jp/content/001018385.pdf.
———. 2022. *Josei no katsuyaku ni kansuru "Jōhō kōhyō" ga kawarimasu* [The information disclosure on the Promotion of Women's Active Engagement will change], accessed Sep 30, 2023, https://www.mhlw.go.jp/content/11900000/001031891.pdf.
———. 2017a. *Tenkin ni kansuru koyō kanri no pointo (kashō) no sakutei ni muketa kenkyūkai, hōkokusho* [Study Group and Report for Deciding "Points of Labor

Management on *Tenkin* (Provisional Title)], accessed Sep 30, 2023, http://www.mhlw.go.jp/file/04-Houdouhappyou-11903000-Koyoukintoujidoukateikyoku-Shokugyoukateiryouritsuka/0000158396.pdf.

———. 2017b. *Heisei 29 nen shūrō jōken sōgō chōsa no gaikyō* [Summary of Comprehensive Study of Labor Conditions], accessed Sep 30, 2023, https://www.mhlw.go.jp/toukei/itiran/roudou/jikan/syurou/17/dl/gaikyou.pdf.

———. 2016. *Josei no shokugyō seikatsu ni okeru katsuyaku no suishin ni kansuru hōritsu no gaiyō* [Summary of Act on the Promotion of Women's Active Engagement in Professional Life], accessed Sep. 30, 2023, https://www.mhlw.go.jp/file/06-Seisakujouhou-11900000-Koyoukintoujidoukateikyoku/0000095826.pdf.

———. 2015. *Naibu kokuhatsu wo keiki to shita shokuba ijime to kaisha no houteki sekinin* [Workplace Bully by Whistle-blowing and Legal Responsibility of the Company], accessed Sep 30, 2023, https://www.no-harassment.mhlw.go.jp/foundation/judicail-precedent/archives/5.

———. 2014. *Dai 7 ji kangoshokuin juyō mitōshi ni tsuite* [The 7th Prospects of Demand of Nurses], accessed Sep 30, 2023, http://www.mhlw.go.jp/file/05-Shingikai-10801000-Iseikyoku-Soumuka/0000067083_1.pdf.

———. 2010. *Kaisei ikuji, kaigo kyūgyō hō no aramashi* [Outline of Revised Child and Family Care Leave Law], accessed Sep 30, 2023, http://www.mhlw.go.jp/topics/2009/07/dl/tp0701-1o.pdf.

Miyoshi, Katsuyo. 2009. *Tenkin to kikon josei no kyaria keisei* [Relocation and Married Women's Career Development]. Tokyo: Hakutō shobou.

Mirza, Vincent. 2016. "Young Women and Social Change in Japan: Family and Marriage in a Time of Upheaval." *Japanese Studies* 36 (1): 21–37.

Morikawa, Hidemasa. 1981. *Nihon keieishi* [Japanese Corporate Business History]. Tokyo: Nikkei shinsho.

Nagase, Nobuko. 2022. "*Shōshika, jinkō genshō wo kokufuku suru tameni hitsuyō na seisaku ni tsuite*" [Policies Necessary to Tackle Fertility and Demographic Decline]. *Josei to keizai benkyōkai* [Study Meeting for Women and Economy], accessed Sep. 30, 2023. https://www.kantei.go.jp/jp/content/000116764.pdf.

Nakazato, Hideki. 2017. "Fathers on Leave Alone in Japan: The Lived Experiences of the Pioneers." In O'Brien, Margaret, and Karin Wall eds., *Comparative Perspectives on Work-Life Balance and Gender Equality: Fathers on Leave Alone*, 231–55. Switzerland: Springer Open.

Nemoto, Kumiko. 2016. *Too Few Women at the Top: The Persistence of Inequality in Japan*. Ithaca: ILR Press.

NPO Fathering Japan. 2024. *Ikubosu kigyō dō mei* [Caring Boss Corporate Alliance], accessed Aug 8, 2024, http://fathering.jp/ikuboss/about/ikuboss-alliance/.

———. 2023. "*FJ towa: FJ no vijon*" [About us: FJ's Vision], accessed Sep 30, 2023, http://fathering.jp/about.

North, Scott. 2014. "Hiding Fatherhood in Corporate Japan." In Inhorn, Marcia C., Chavking Wendy, and Navarrro Jose-Alberto, eds., *Globalized Fatherhood*, 53–77. New York and Oxford: Berghahn Books.

———. 2009. "Negotiating What's 'Natural': Persistent Domestic Gender Role Inequality in Japan." *Social Science Japan Journal* 12 (1): 23–44.

Nosaka, Akiko. 2012. "Aspirations and Desires: Women's Education and Fertility Strategies in Contemporary Japan." *Human Organization* 71 (2): 188–99.
Ochiai, Emiko. 1994. *21 seiki kazoku e* [For 21st century family]. Tokyo: Yuikaku.
Ogasawara, Yuko. 1998. *Office Ladies and Salaried Men: Power, Gender, and Work in Japanese Companies.* Berkeley, California: University of California Press.
Okifuji, Noriko. 1991. *Tenkin zoku no tsuma tachi* [Wives of transfer tribes]. Tokyo: Kōdansha.
Ortner, Sherry. 2006. *Anthropology and Social Theory: Culture, Power, and the Acting Subject.* Durham: Duke University Press.
———. 1984. "Theory in Anthropology since the Sixties." *Comparative Studies in Society and History* 26 (1): 126–66.
Ōsawa, Mari. 1993. *Kigyō chūshin shakai wo koete: Gendai shakai wo jendā de yomu* [Beyond the Corporate-centered Society: Reading Contemporary Society through Gender]. Tokyo: Jijitsūshin.
Pucik, Vladimir. 1984. "White-Collar Human Resource Management in Large Japanese Manufacturing Firms." *Human Resource Management* 23 (3): 257–76.
Rebick, Marcus. 2005. *The Japanese Employment System: Adapting to a New Economic Environment.* Oxford: Oxford University Press.
Roberts, Glenda S. 2020. "Leaning *Out* for the Long Span: What Holds Women Back from Promotion in Japan?." *Japan Forum* 32 (4): 555–76.
———. 2016. *Japan's Evolving Family: Voices from Young Urban Adults Navigating Change.* Hawaii: East-west Center.
———. 2014. "Work and Life in Challenging Times: A Kansai Family Across the Generations." In Kawano, Satsuki, Glenda S. Roberts, and Susan Orpett Long eds., *Capturing Contemporary Japan: Differentiation and Uncertainty,* 27–59. Honolulu: University of Hawaii Press.
———. 2011. "Salary Women and Family Well-Being in Urban Japan." *Marriage and Family Review* 47 (8): 571–89.
———. 2005. "Balancing Work and Life: Whose Work, Whose Life, Whose Balance?" *Journal of Asia-Pacific Studies* 7: 61–84.
———. 1994. *Staying on the Line: Blue-collar Women in Contemporary Japan.* Honolulu: University of Hawaii Press.
Roberts, Glenda S. and Hiroko Costantini. 2023. "The Work, Family, and Care Nexus in Paris and Tokyo: Gender Equality and Well-Being among Urban Professionals." *Contemporary Japan* 35 (2): 214–47.
Rohlen, Thomas P. 1974. *For Harmony and Strength: Japanese White-Collar Organization in Anthropological Perspective.* Berkley: University of California Press.
Rosenbaum, James E. 1979. "Tournament Mobility: Career Patterns in a Corporation." *Administrative Science Quarterly* 24 (2): 220–41.
Rosenberger, Nancy. 2013. *Dilemmas of Adulthood: Japanese Women and the Nuances of Long-term Resistance.* Honolulu: University of Hawaii Press.
———. 2001. *Gambling with Virtue: Japanese Women and the Search for Self in a Changing Nation.* Honolulu: University of Hawaii Press.

Sahlins, Marshall. 1981. *Historical Metaphors and Mythical Realities: Structure in the Early History of the Sandwich Islands Kingdom.* Ann Arbor: The University of Michigan Press.

Saitō, Osamu. 2006. "Bushi to tedai: Tokugawa nihon no 'seishain.'" [Samurai and Sales Person: 'Regular Employees' in the Tokugawa period of Japan. *Nihon Rōdō Kenkyū Zasshi* 552: 60–6.

———. 2002. *Edo to Osaka: Kindai nihon no toshi kigen* [Edo and Osaka: The Birth of Urban City in Modern Japan]. Tokyo: NTT publications.

Sankei Shimbun. 2018. "*AIG sonpo, tenkin tomonau idō haishi e: Tenkin ooi kinyū gyōkai ni isseki*" [AIG General Insurance Abolishing Transfers Accompanying *Tenkin*: A sensation to the Financial Industry with Frequent *Tenkin*], accessed Sep. 30, 2023, https://www.sankei.com/economy/news/180212/ecn1802120005-n1.html.

Sato, Kaori, Yuki Hashimoto, and Hideo Owan. 2019. "Gender Differences in Career." *Journal of The Japanese and International Economics* 53: 1–13.

Schein, Edgar H. 1991. *Organizational Culture and Leadership.* San Francisco: Jossey-Bass Publishers.

Schoppa, Leonard J. 2006. *Race for the Exits: The Unraveling of Japan's System of Social Protection.* Ithaca; New York: Cornell University Press.

Senda, Sachiko, and Ōuchi Akiko. 2002. "*Josei seiki jūgyōin no kyaria keisei no tayōsei: kōsu betsu koyō kanri seido wo tegakari toshite*" [Diversity of career development of women regular workers: Learned from course-based employment management system]. *Soshiki kagaku* 36 (1): 95–107.

Sewell, William H Jr. 1992. "A Theory of Structure: Duality, Agency, and Transformation." *American Journal of Sociology* 98 (1): 1–29.

Shimpo, Hiroshi, and Saitō Osamu eds. 1989. *Nihon keizaishi 2: Kindai seichō no taidō* [Japanese Economic History: Signs of Modern Development]. Tokyo: Iwanami shoten.

Soma, Naoko, and Yamashita Junko. 2020. "*Nihon ni okeru chūkōnen josei no daburu kea to seidoteki fuseigi: Fukushi seisaku to tōjisha no kōshō katei ni kansuru jirei bunseki kara.*" [Double Care of Middle-aged Women and Systematic Injustice in Japan: Welfare Policy and Case Analysis on Negotiation Process of the Actors]. *Ohara Shakai Mondai Kenkyujo Zasshi* 737: 33–51.

Sugayama, Shinji. 2011. *"Shūsha" shakai no tanjō: howaito karā kara burū karā e* [The birth of "society entering into company": From white-collar to blue-collar]. Nagoya: Nagoya daigaku shuppankai.

Tabata, Hirokuni. 1998. "Community and Efficiency in the Japanese Firm." *Social Science Japan Journal* 1 (2): 199–215.

Tanaka, Yūko. 2002. *Tanshin funin to shinriteki sutoresu: kazoku bunri ni tsuiteno jisshōteki kōsatsu* [Solo transfer and psychological stress: An empirical study of family separation]. Kyoto: Nakanishiya shuppan.

———. 1991. *Tanshin funin no kenkyū* [A study of solo transfer]. Tokyo: Chūō keizaisha.

Tōyō Keizai Online. 2016. "*Ikuji shain eno hairyo yamemasu: Shiseido no ito*" [We will stop considering child-caring workers: An intention of Shiseido], accessed Sep. 30, 2023, https://toyokeizai.net/articles/-/104831.

Tōyō Keizai Shinpōsha. 2014. *Shūshoku Shikihō* [Corporate Quarterly Report for Recruitment].

Tsuji, Katsuji. 2011. *Toyota jinji hōshiki no sengo shi: Kigyō shakai no hatten kara shūen made* [The Postwar History of Toyota Personnel System: From Development of Corporate-oriented Society to the End]. Kyoto: Minerva shobō.

Ueno, Chizuko. 2009. *Kafuchō sei to shihon sei: Marukusu shugi feminizumu no chihei* [The Patriarchy and Capitalism: Ground of Marxist Feminism. Tokyo: Iwanami shoten.

Vogel, Suzanne Hall. 2013. *The Japanese Family in Transition: From the Professional Housewife Ideal to the Dilemmas of Choice.* Lanham, Maryland: Rowman and Littlefield Publishers, Inc.

Watsuji, Tetsuro. 1961. *A Climate: A Philosophical Study.* Tokyo: Printing Bureau, Japanese Government.

WEF [World Economic Forum]. 2023. GGGR [Global Gender Gap Report], accessed Sep. 30, 2023, https://www3.weforum.org/docs/WEF_GGGR_2023.pdf.

White, Merry Isaacs. 2002. *Perfectly Japanese: Making Families in and Era of Upheaval.* Berkeley: University of California Press.

Yamamoto, Kiyoshi. 1967. *Nihon rōdō shijō no kōzō: "gijutsu kakushin" to rōdō shijō no kōzōtekihenka* [Structure of the Japanese labor market: "Technological innovation" and structural change of the labor market]. Tokyo: Tokyo daigaku shuppankai.

Yashiro, Atsushi. 1995. *Daikigyō howaito karā no kyaria: idō to shōshin no jisshō bunseki* [White-collar careers at large companies: An empirical analysis of transfer and promotion]. Tokyo: Rōdō seisaku kenkyū kenshū kikō.

Yomiuri Shimbun. 2021. *"Korona ka, Hatarakikata kaikaku de tenkin ha dounaru"* [Under the COVID-19 Does the Reform of Working Style Affect *Tenkin*], accessed Sep 30, 2023, https://www.yomiuri.co.jp/column/henshu/20211118-OYT8T50056/.

Index

ability, 8, 13, 14, 34, 36, 45, 47, 59, 104, 107, 126, 140
accompanying, 46, 48, 49, 54, 55
Act on the Promotion of Women's Active Engagement in Professional Life [*Josei Katsuyaku Suishin Hō*], 4, 50
agency, 5–7, 27, 74, 101, 113, 123, 125, 127, 132, 136

babysitter, 95–97, 116
biological clock, 89, 109
blue-collar: employment, 11, 13, 79; worker/employees, 10, 12, 17, 19, 41, 81, 136
bosei hogo [protection of women], 33
breadwinner, 2–4, 16, 20, 31, 48–54, 57, 77, 78, 98, 101, 107, 137

capacity, 5
career development, 2, 17, 31, 37–38, 60, 65
career management, 27–28, 135, 141
chūzai, 66, 103, 133
communication skill, 60–61, 90, 113, 122
company housing, 46, 105
consent [*dōi*], 40, 43

course-based hiring/employment system, 17, 43, 84
custom, 8, 13, 16, 27, 31, 37–41, 54–55, 63, 137, 139–40

diversity and inclusion, 57, 61–64, 121, 137
dual-career [*tomobataraki*] couple/family, 1–4, 13, 20, 22, 24, 27–28

Edo, 8, 75, 136
efficiency, 8, 12, 13, 14, 16, 27, 34, 38, 49, 52, 54–55, 65, 123, 126, 129, 130, 137
elder care, 15, 19, 49, 56, 129, 132
equity, 62
exemption/exempt [*menjo*], 3, 22, 53, 80

fairness, 53, 62, 63, 69, 124, 128, 129, 130, 140
fertility, 2, 82, 85–87
fūdo [climate], 36, 37, 55, 61

Global Gender Gap Index 4
global business/economy, 22, 33, 37, 57, 58, 63, 64, 122, 137, 140
good reasons, 39, 40, 69, 120, 139

haichi, 34, 52

hairyo [consider, consideration], 3, 15, 35, 45, 69, 82, 98
homemaker, 2, 16, 20, 49, 77, 78, 90, 98, 101, 104, 137, 138
human capability, 6, 64, 138
human resource (HR) development, 2, 31, 34, 35, 51, 103, 136, 137, 139, 140, 144

idō, 32, 38, 46, 55
ie, 28, 78, 80, 88
Ikubosu [caring bosses], 26, 128–33
independence, 79, 131, 138, 139
Internal Labor Market (ILM), 7–18, 27, 28, 31–55, 63, 136, 137, 141

job hunting, 26, 27, 46, 56, 66, 70, 73, 111, 133

Law: Child and Family Care Leave, 3, 15, 68; Equal Employment Opportunity, 17, 33; Labor Standard, 33, 39–41
leave system: childcare, 56, 91, 92, 94, 95, 96, 102–18, 120; following, 62, 77, 115, 122, 124–25, 144; maternity, 91, 95, 103; self-enlightenment, 111–12

marital relationship, 22, 27, 79, 83, 85, 86, 88, 89, 90, 92, 93, 94, 95, 101–25, 138–39
Meiji, 8, 78, 98
mommy track, 96, 112

naiji [unofficial announcement], 36, 38
negotiation: inter-personal-(in workplace/home), 7, 27, 36, 37, 60, 61, 63, 64, 87, 95, 98, 108, 113, 118–23, 124, 130–31, 132, 138, 139–40; labor-management-/collective-, 41, 42

on-the-job training (OJT), 8, 31, 32, 34, 54

reform: labor market-, 28, 139–40; organizational-/personnel, 42, 43, 44, 50, 53; of *tenkin* (-related) practices, 58–61, 141; of the working style, 2, 159
Reiwa, 4, 135, 140, 141

salariiman/men, 65, 67, 70, 74, 90
Shōwa, 4, 129, 135, 136, 141
skill specificity, 8, 31, 34, 54, 63
string along, 38, 46, 47
structure, 18, 21, 65, 74, 108, 123, 136, 138; employment-, 13, 64, 98; family-, 47, 78, 80, 81, 122, 135; social-, 5–7, 13, 16; *tenkin*-/-of *tenkin*, 28, 46, 137

tenshoku, 1

union, 9, 12, 13, 15, 18, 35, 37, 41–42, 48, 57, 62, 63, 87, 137, 140
unlimited (in working styles incl. *tenkin*), 38, 43, 96

white-collar: crimes, 56, 140; dual-career couples, 135; jobs, 20; workers/employees, 8–13, 16, 17, 32, 67, 127, 136; workplaces 31, 42
work/life or work-life, 2, 25, 26, 52, 53, 56, 66, 76, 96, 97, 128, 132, 135
work rules, 14, 28, 32, 37, 39–43, 45–46, 54, 55, 139

yome [bride], 28, 78, 79, 80
yuchaku [adhesion], 38, 71

About the Author

Noriko Fujita, PhD, is assistant professor at College of Humanities, Tamagawa University, Tokyo. Her ethnographic research focuses on gender, labor, family, migrant policies, DE&I, and animal ethics in contemporary Japan. Her publication includes "Corporate Transfers for Dual-Career Couples: From Gendered *Tenkin* to Gender-Equal Negotiations?" (2021), "Engagement among Pet-Industry Agents: What 'Human-Pet Coexistence' Means in Japan (2023)" and "Low-skilled Migrant Labor Schemes in Japan's Agriculture: Voices from the Field" (2024).

Milton Keynes UK
Ingram Content Group UK Ltd.
UKHW041524171024
449876UK00004B/30